VENUS & SERENA
The Grand Slam Williams Sisters

VENUS & SERENA

The Grand Slam Williams Sisters

by Bill Gutman

SCHOLASTIC INC.

New York Toronto London Auckland Sydney
Mexico City New Delhi Hong Kong

Photo credits:

ISBN 0-439-27152-5

12 11 10 9 8 7 6 5 4 3 2 1   1 2 3 4 5/0

Printed in the U.S.A.   40

First Scholastic printing, January 2001

Contents

VENUS & SERENA
The Grand Slam Williams Sisters

Introduction:
Sisters and Champions

Nearly every time they walk onto a tennis court, Venus and Serena Williams are making history. They are the first sisters ever to be ranked among the best players in the world and the first sisters to have each won a Grand Slam singles championship. The best part is that older sister Venus won her first Slam, the 2000 Wimbledon championship, shortly after turning twenty years old. Younger sister Serena won the 1999 U.S. Open championship at the age of eighteen! In other words, their tennis careers have just begun.

But winning isn't the only thing that makes the Williams sisters two of the most unique and charismatic athletes in the world. They are revolutionizing the sport of tennis in many ways. They grew up in the dangerous, drug-infested ghetto area of Compton, California. They are also African-American women who are playing in a traditionally white sport. Most young tennis hopefuls learn to play at posh country clubs or pay-as-you-go city courts, which were places the Williams sisters could not access in Compton.

Black tennis champions have been few and far between. The two most famous, Althea Gibson and Arthur Ashe, both had to contend with many episodes of racism during their careers. Despite this history, Richard Williams, Venus and Serena's father, decided to help his daughters go for it. He began teaching his two youngest daughters tennis when they were barely old enough to hold a racket. He was their coach, yet his only knowledge of the sport came from reading books and watching videos. He knew the odds and knew what his daughters would face. From the beginning, he decided to do it his way.

That's what makes the Williamses' story even more amazing. Richard Williams didn't always do things in the conventional manner. He never pushed his two daughters. Both Venus and Serena loved tennis and the competion from the very first day they hit a ball. Nor did he stress tennis to the exclusion of everything else. In fact, Mr. Williams always made sure education was their number-one priority. He gave his daughters a strong sense of who they are. They learned about history, about people, about racism, about being black in a predominantly white world. He and his wife also made sure their daughters had a wide variety of interests. In other words, if Venus and Serena didn't become tennis stars, there would be many other ways for them to go.

As it turned out, both Venus and Serena Williams did become champions. In doing so, they have brought something new and exciting to women's tennis. Both girls are not only great tennis players but great athletes as well. They play a power game never before seen in women's tennis. Strong and extremely quick, the sisters are improving every year. Both sisters are ranked in the top ten in the world. In the minds of many, the day isn't far off when they will be numbers one and two.

The Williamses' meteoric rise in the tennis world brings about another situation never before seen in an individual sport. These two loving sisters, who are best friends and extremely close, sometimes find themselves facing each other for top prizes in tennis. Having to battle each other where just one person can win may be their toughest hurdle yet. But both girls have shown themselves to be so confident and well adjusted that they get through this challenge easily.

The rise of Venus and Serena Williams has not been without controversy. Early in their careers, the girls were often accused of being aloof and not friendly enough. Because they didn't fall in with the mainstream right away, others viewed them with suspicion. Yet they have persevered, and now they are among the most popular players on the Tour. And maybe the best.

It is really a Cinderella story with a twist. Here

there are two Cinderellas, a pair of girls who are on an unbelievable journey. In tennis, the story of teenage sensations hasn't always had happy endings. With Venus and Serena Williams, it's hard to see it ending any other way.

1
On the Courts at Compton

To fully understand how the story of Venus and Serena Williams began, you have to know about their father, Richard. He was the son of a Louisiana cotton sharecropper, which gave him a firsthand glimpse at a way of life that went back more than one hundred years. As a sharecropper, his mother had to work extremely hard to eke out a meager living.

"[She worked] too hard," he said many years later. "She was too good at what she did."

Apparently, being good at something made an impression on young Richard, because he would carry it with him always. He began working hard as a young boy. There was little time for much else. When other boys his age began playing baseball, football, or basketball, Richard Williams continued to work. The closest he ever came to playing sports was his experience caddying at a local golf club. He sometimes got to play a few rounds after caddying, but he never pursued the sport.

Oracene Williams, Venus and Serena's mother, came from a very different background. She was the daughter of a corporate executive and a university official in Michigan. Later, she moved to Mississippi to work as a nurse. Just after Richard and Oracene married, Richard began to have hopes for the future. He knew virtually nothing about tennis, but he recalled watching a tournament in the late 1970s in which the winner's prize was $30,000 or $40,000.

"She won that money after playing for just four days," he said. "And I thought, 'What a living that could be for a female.'"

Soon, Richard and Brandi (Oracene's nickname) began having daughters. Lyndrea came first, then Isha, and next Yetunde. During this time, the family moved several times, looking for a place to establish themselves. When Venus was born on June 17, 1980, the family was living in Lynwood, California. Some fifteen months later, on September 26, 1981, in Saginaw, Michigan, Serena became daughter number five. Shortly after Serena was born, Richard Williams had a plan for how he wanted to raise his daughters.

He insisted on moving the family into one of the roughest areas in the country, the inner-city neighborhood of Compton, California. Mrs. Williams didn't think this was a very good idea, but Richard Williams persisted. He felt his children should be raised tough, that it would better prepare them to deal with the real world.

"My wife said I was bringing up the kids the

wrong way," Mr. Williams said. "But my mom brought me up to be responsible. I don't know when I started working. When [the girls] reached the age of two, I wanted them to work, and my wife said, 'That's not going to happen.'"

Richard Williams didn't change his mind about raising the girls in Compton. The area had some problems with gangs, drive-by shootings, and drugs. The family didn't have to live there. Mrs. Williams was working as a nurse, and Mr. Williams eventually ran a private security firm. The family could afford to live elsewhere. But they stayed by choice.

Mr. Williams continued to think about tennis. A great player could make a lot of money, but thousands of young girls played the game around the country and very few could go on to be great players. But Richard Williams stuck with the plan. When his girls were just two years old, he had them lifting and delivering phone books to build up their muscles. One way or another, he had them working.

All the while, he continued to watch tennis on television. He read about the sport and bought instructional videos. When each of his girls was just past the age of four, he began taking them out to the local tennis courts and had them hitting balls. None of the first three Williams girls really took to the sport. Mr. Williams would bring a shopping cart filled with five hundred fifty tennis balls onto the court. Each girl had to hit all the balls before they could go home. Lyndrea, Isha, and Yetunde took forever to go through the cart, as did other neighborhood girls who came out to play. It was obvious that they weren't really enjoying it. None of the three oldest girls made it look like Richard's dream had a chance of coming true.

Then along came Venus. When she was about four and a half, her father took her out to the courts for the first time. Her attitude was completely different from that of her older sisters. Richard Williams said he saw something special that first day. "While the other kids were taking a break [from hitting], Venus wanted to hit every ball in that basket," Mr. Williams said. "She wouldn't stop. Every time you tried to stop her, she would start crying. She was only four years old. That doesn't mean she hit every ball. A lot of them she missed. But she would swing at every ball. When she got to the last ball in the basket, she told me to say, 'Last one,' and I said, 'Okay, last one.' And to this day, I say the same thing to her when she's practicing."

It was the same every day after that. Venus couldn't wait to go through the hundreds of balls. She hit them with a smile on her face. As soon as she hit one, she got ready to hit another, then another.

In fact, Mr. Williams remembers bringing Venus home that first day and immediately telling his wife, "We have a winner. She said, 'How do you know?' I told her Venus demonstrated all four qualities of a champion. No matter what age, all champions are able to demonstrate that they are rough, they are tough, they are strong, and they are mentally sound. You cannot teach that. That is a God-given quality, and Venus demonstrated that on the first day."

Whether it happened that way is hard to say. But one thing is certain: Venus Williams was a tennis player from day one. Those qualities of a champion would continue to be evident in upcoming years.

The three oldest Williams girls were encouraged to concentrate solely on their education. Venus was the tennis player. Of course, she had to concentrate on her education, as well. That was always the number-one priority. Venus knew that if she did poorly in school, there would be no tennis. Poorly, to Richard Williams, was anything less than an A. The one thing Venus didn't want was to have tennis taken away, so she always worked as hard in school as on the courts.

Of course, there was another Williams daughter standing on the sidelines. Mr. Williams waited until Serena was about four and a half, like her sisters, before taking her out to the courts with Venus. Suddenly, there were two. Serena took to the game almost immediately. She quickly showed the tenacity and competitiveness that would become her trademark. Older sister Lyndrea confirmed that her two sisters were naturals. "Venus and Serena took to tennis as soon as rackets were put in their hands," she said.

Venus and Serena accompanied their father to the courts every day, hitting ball after ball and already beginning to compete with each other. "To this day," their father said, "Venus is Serena's hero and best friend. Venus definitely set the stage for Serena."

Being fifteen months older and having started sooner, Venus was more advanced than her sister in those early years. But she continually drove her sister to keep up with her, to compete with her, and young Serena responded. She worked very hard because she wanted to be as good as her sister.

Growing up in inner-city Compton wasn't easy or safe. Though none of the Williams girls ever got in trouble, trouble was never very far away. Even practicing tennis could be dangerous. Venus remembers a day when she was about eight or nine when tennis practice turned into something else. "We were practicing on the court in East Compton Park," she said, "when someone raised up and started shooting. I don't know what they were shooting at. The courts were right by the street. We all just dived for cover."

That was probably a frightening experience, but it didn't deter the girls or their father. Practice was something they did no matter what was going on around them. In a way, Richard Williams had been right about Compton. Living there and persevering, despite the problems in the area, would eventually make both girls stronger.

Soon the sisters were playing in local age-group tournaments and winning. Mrs. Williams recalls the first match the sisters played against each other. "There was a tournament at Indian Wells when we were still living in California," she recalled. "Venus was entered, but Serena wasn't supposed to be in it. She decided to enter herself, even filled out all the forms. She was just eight years old then. When she told me she was in the tournament I said, 'No, you're not.' She told me to check with the organizers. There she was, in the tournament. So she played and made it all the way to the finals, where she wound up losing to Venus."

It became apparent that Richard Williams's early assessment of his girls' ability might not have been as far-fetched as some people thought. The girls were sweeping through age-group competitions and winning most of their junior matches, which were sanctioned by the United States Tennis Association (USTA). First Venus, then Serena, was ranked number one in the southern California twelve-and-under rankings. It was a competitive group, with many fine players. But Venus and Serena had begun to shine.

In fact, the Sanex Women's Tennis Association (WTA) player profile states that by age twelve, Venus had accumulated a 63-0 record in USTA sectional play in southern California. Richard Williams claims that Serena won forty-six of the forty-nine tournaments she entered in the first five years she played.

So it certainly seemed as if Richard and Brandi Williams had done their jobs well. As Venus was about to turn twelve and Serena was going on eleven, it appeared that both were headed for stardom. Many young women have turned pro at a very young age, though that practice was coming under closer scrutiny. So the question was which way their parents would take the girls.

11

Over the next few years, Richard Williams made a number of controversial choices for the two sisters, choices that surprised a lot of people. Many felt that Mr. Williams was hurting his daughters' chances to become tennis stars. Richard Williams had his own timetable, however, and felt in his heart that what he was doing was right.

2
Tennis Isn't the Only Thing

The road to the women's professional tennis tour has been filled with teenage sensations planning to take the court world by storm. There's no doubt that some girls at age thirteen, fourteen, or fifteen were good enough to compete on the tour and play against the best. Some, however, have met with early success only to see the road turn ugly. The three biggest roadblocks in tennis to continued success are injury, burnout, and too much parental control.

In the late 1970s and early 1980s, two teenage girls were among the best players in the world. Tracy Austin and Andrea Jaeger both joined the tour full-time at age fourteen. Austin won the U.S. Open twice, in 1979 and again in 1981. Jaeger never won a Grand Slam championship but was ranked in the top five for several years. Both girls eventually had their careers end prematurely because of nagging injuries. Some began to feel that the stresses young players were putting on their bodies were just too great. They were still grow-ing, and the constant wear and tear was bound to produce serious injuries. Today, players turning pro at an early age cannot play in World Tennis Association events until they are sixteen.

Burnout is another problem young players face. Those who showed championship potential at an early age were sometimes driven to play and prac-tice constantly. Their lives consisted of tennis and little else. One such player was Jennifer Capriati, who burst on the scene as a thirteen-year-old in 1990. Capriati amazed the tennis world with her skills and tenacity, and it seemed that she was on her way to becoming one of the best. But just a few short years later she rebelled and left tennis. She was tired of not having any fun and being pressured into a tennis-only life.

Controlling parents, especially tennis fathers, have been another ongoing problem on the tour. There are parents who, looking at the increasing amounts of prize money available at the various tournaments, see their daughters as cash cows. So they drive their children harder, looking at their own pocketbooks and not worrying about the physical and emotional well-being of the teenager forced to live in the pressure cooker that is big-time tennis.

These were the things that Richard and Brandi Williams had to consider as their two daughters continued to win and improve on the junior tennis circuit. Mr. Williams decided to pull his daughters off the national junior circuit. That was contro-versial move number one.

The junior circuit is where most young players develop and refine the skills they need to compete as professionals against older, more experienced players. It was the path to stardom for young players. Yet Richard Williams told his daughters he didn't want them playing on the circuit anymore. Venus was nearly twelve at the time, and Serena was going on eleven.

Of course, Mr. Williams had his reasons. He wanted to make sure his daughters concentrated on their schoolwork. He believed that should always come first. There were other reasons for his decision as well. He said that he didn't want to subject his daughters to a heavy dose of competitive pressure at this point in their careers. The emphasis was on winning in the junior circuit, and he felt there would be plenty of time for that later. Too much pressure, he felt, and it would be the schoolwork that would suffer. He also wanted his daughters to be well-rounded individuals. He didn't want them to think that the entire world was contained between the lines on a tennis court.

Mr. Williams also said he wanted to be sure that his young daughters were not subjected to an undertone of racial hostility. It was assumed that he was just being careful. But with so few African-Americans playing on the junior circuit and in the pros, there was bound to be some hostility. In fact, he later talked about a time when Venus was younger and playing in an age-group tournament in southern California and faced early prejudice.

Venus wasn't yet a household name, and everyone at the match assumed that, being black, she was poor. "I overheard some people say we shouldn't even be there," Richard Williams recalled. "They said we were from Compton and that we shouldn't even be there. 'They can't play,' someone said. People would pick at us all the time. There comes a time when you get tired of people picking on you."

Mr. Williams wanted to be sure his daughters were ready for this kind of thing. He wanted them to be old enough, smart enough, and talented enough to deal with it. If that meant pulling them out of the juniors, so be it. Later, he would admit that his master plan had a purpose. "I came out of the worst ghetto in the world and was simply trying to prove to the world that it doesn't matter where you come from to be good in tennis," he explained. "You don't have to be brought up in the country club to do this. You can actually come out of the ghetto and play tennis."

Some people have been quick to criticize Mr. Williams for certain statements. He has been accused of exaggeration, of seeing things only from his point of view. But whatever he did seemed to be for the eventual good of his daughters.

"Over a period of time," he said, "we gained so much confidence in what we were trying to do. A person can pick at you so long, enough that, instead of making you weak, it makes you strong. We decided that we just didn't care what people thought. That only thing that would matter in the end was what [we] thought."

After he pulled Venus and Serena out of competition, their father devised a new plan. To get better they could no longer stay in Compton and play on the local courts. He sent both girls to the Florida tennis academy of Ric Macci. Macci was a teaching pro who had worked with many young players, notably Jennifer Capriati and Mary Pierce. Shortly after the girls went to Florida, the rest of the family followed, settling in Palm Beach Gardens. Venus and Serena continued to love the game and work very hard at it in Florida.

"Venus just didn't come out of the streets of Compton and suddenly have all these great strokes," Ric Macci said. "She worked six hours a day, six days a week. There wasn't a day that the girl wouldn't hit two hundred serves." And of course, whatever Venus did, Serena did also.

After some time in Florida, their father decided he didn't want the girls to go through regular channels in life. In 1993 he pulled both of them out of the Florida school system and began educating them at home. Venus would eventually get her diploma from a private school in 1997, finishing with a 3.8 grade average. Serena followed suit a short time later.

On the tennis front he didn't let things slide, either. Though both girls improved their games working under Ric Macci, the association didn't last long. Richard Williams and Macci didn't agree about the number of tournaments the girls should play. In addition, Mr. Williams always wanted a hand in coaching. That wouldn't work, so Macci was gone. The girls studied briefly with another famous coach, Nick Bollettieri, but that didn't last long, either. Coaching the girls always came back to Mr. Williams. Yet even Nick Bollettieri didn't think that was such a bad thing. A few years later, he said, "Nobody knows those girls better than their parents. The road they've gone on couldn't have been better selected."

3
Turning Pro

Despite the controversy and the questionable moves made by their father, there was still very little known about Venus and Serena Williams in the early 1990s. Those who followed women's tennis closely knew who they were. But because their father had pulled them out of the juniors, no one really knew about their game and how they were progressing. They certainly weren't expected to make an impact on the tennis world anytime soon.

For that reason, it was a real surprise when Richard Williams announced that Venus would become a professional. The date was October 31, 1994, a little more than four months after her fourteenth birthday. Why, people wondered, would a man who was as cautious as Richard Williams have his daughter turn pro at fourteen? After all, Venus hadn't even played much in the juniors. To the tennis world, Richard Williams wasn't making any sense. But as usual, Mr. Williams had a plan. He and his daughter would do it their way.

Women's tennis had come a long way over the past two decades. There had been great champions in the early years but not nearly as many as in recent years. Suzanne Lenglen of France and Helen Wills Moody of the United States both became tennis legends in the 1920s and 1930s. The two dominated the women's game, winning many tournaments and Grand Slam titles. In 1951, a sixteen-year-old American named Maureen Connolly made tennis history by winning the U.S. Open. "Little Mo" dominated for several years until a horseback riding accident ended her career in 1954.

Three years later more history was made in women's tennis. Althea Gibson, a black woman born in Silver, South Carolina, had learned the game by playing paddle tennis in New York City. In 1956, she won the French Open, then in 1957 and 1958, she became the first African-American to win both Wimbledon and the U.S. Open. She won each twice.

By the 1960s and into the 1970s, two women players dominated the game, Margaret Smith Court of Australia and Billie Jean King of the United States. Both won a slew of Grand Slam titles. Women players were coming into their own in other ways as well. Led by King, many women on the tour began demanding more money. At that time, they were earning a third of what the corresponding men's champions were getting. A number of the top players left the USTA tour and formed one of their own. Out of that new league came the Virginia Slims Tour and the Sanex WTA Tour.

King made huge strides for women's tennis in 1973 when she played a former men's champion. Bobby Riggs, who had already beaten Margaret Court and claimed that no woman could beat a man, even one twenty years her senior, played King in the Houston Astrodome on September 20, before 30,472 fans. Many more watched on national television. It was the largest crowd ever to watch a tennis match. King was brilliant. She defeated Riggs in three straight sets. Women's tennis was now fully on the map. The prize money in major tournaments had become comparable.

More great players continued to come into the game. Chris Evert was the first champion to use the two-hand backhand, and she played a brilliant baseline game. A few years later Evert found herself challenged by Martina Navratilova. Born in Czechoslovakia, Navratilova eventually became a United States citizen. She also played a power game not seen in women's tennis before. Her serve was timed at ninety-three miles per hour, and she often used a serve-and-volley game: She would charge the net after serving and pick off the return for an easy winner. She and Evert had a great rivalry for a number of years. When she retired, Navratilova had won a record nine Wimbledon singles championships, among her many other accomplishments.

The champions kept coming. By the late 1980s and early 1990s, Steffi Graf and Monica Seles were dominating the women's game. In the middle 1990s, a whole new group of young players was about to emerge — including Venus Williams. Women's tennis had become big business, with millions of dollars in prize money available, not to mention millions more in commercial endorsement deals for the best and most popular players.

When Venus turned pro at fourteen, many thought she would be sent onto the court as many times as she was allowed. Maybe, people thought, Richard Williams was ready to cash in on his daughter's talent. But that wasn't the plan. Mr. Williams felt he had not one but two future champions, and he wasn't about to throw them to the wolves. Once more, Richard Williams would do it his way. As always, his daughters followed his advice. They both knew he had their best interests at heart.

Although Venus turned pro at fourteen, she played in only a few tournaments early in her career. She was still too young to play in WTA-sanctioned events. She played in just one tournament in 1994. It was held in Oakland. In her first ever professional match, Venus defeated fifty-ninth-ranked Shaun Stafford in straight sets, 6–3, 6–4. In the next round she lost to the world's second-ranked player, Arantxa Sanchez-Vicario, in three sets. Venus won the first, 6–3, and had a 3–0 lead in the second before Sanchez-Vicario rallied to win the match.

Venus continued to practice, mostly with Serena, and go to school. In 1995, she played in just three tournaments, reaching the quarterfinals in only one of them. That October, Serena joined her sister. She, too, was allowed to turn pro at the age of fourteen.

Serena made her debut at the non-WTA Bell Challenge in Vanier, Quebec, Canada. It was a long way to travel for a quick loss. She was beaten in two straight sets and in less than an hour by a virtually unknown player. Nevertheless, it was a start. The next year, 1996, Venus played in five tournaments, losing in the early rounds of all of them. At the end of the year she was the 204th-ranked women's player in the world. Serena played in just a couple of tournaments and wasn't even ranked. The Williams sisters were still unknowns. Only their father was predicting that they would be champions.

But making an immediate impact wasn't in his plans. He was careful not to risk burnout with his daughters and wanted to be sure they didn't lose track of their education. In a sense, Venus and Serena were now on the doorstep. It wouldn't be long before they did a lot more than simply knock on that door. They were about to kick it in.

4
The Williams Mystique
Begins

Even before they began to win steadily, the Williams sisters brought something new to their sport. Things were just different about them — the game they played, their appearance, and their demeanor. Up to this point, the girls had had very little contact with the press. No one really knew them except through their father. People wondered if Venus and Serena would ever make their mark.

Both girls had grown into imposing athletes. Venus was 6 feet 1 inch, with long arms and legs, and weighed more than 160 pounds. Serena had a shorter, blockier build, at 5 feet 10 inches and 145 pounds. But she was becoming very muscular and athletic. Despite their size, both were very quick on the court, moving with grace and purpose.

They also played a power game. Both were developing booming serves, which they already hit harder than most of the girls on the tour. They were right-handed players who used the two-hand backhand, which they combined with a powerful, one-hand forehand. At this stage in their careers, they played mostly from the baseline, toward the rear of the court. It takes a while to learn when to charge the net. A player must gauge the tempo of the game and the way her opponent is playing and keep in mind the score at the time. In addition, the player must anticipate what his or her opponent is going to do. These are things people felt would take a long time for the Williamses to learn. Not playing in the juniors, people reasoned, would hold them back.

There was one other thing that defined the Williams sisters. Whenever Venus or Serena took to the court, they had their hair braided with eighteen hundred beads in a process that took ten hours. On the court, the beads would rattle, causing some opponents to complain. There were several times when a strand would give way, causing the beads to fall onto the court and holding up the match. Their beads were one reason many of the other tour players resented the Williams sisters when they began to play regularly in 1997.

Another thing other players disliked about Venus and Serena was the girls' demeanor. Although they were now around the other players on a regular basis, they were not always friendly. Perhaps it was a carryover from the us-against-them mentality that Richard Williams had instilled in them years earlier. They had been insulated from most of the tennis world for so long that perhaps it was difficult for them to trust the motives of other players.

Lindsay Davenport, who was becoming one of the best players on the Tour, recalled seeing Venus in March 1997 at a tournament at Indian Wells. "I said hello, and she went 'Pooosh,'" Davenport said. "I learned not to do that again."

Monica Seles, another great champion, had a similar experience with Venus. "I once said to Venus, 'Hi,' and she didn't say it back," Seles said. "She seems to be going all the time with her sister, her mom, too. That's what family is for. They stay in their own little separate group."

Venus never made excuses, but there was obviously some degree of suspicion. One time during those early days on the Tour, she told a reporter, "A lot of people don't understand what I am and don't want to know. And I don't know why their lives revolve around me anyway. I don't come to tournaments to make friends, to go to parties, to hold conversations. I come to be the best, and I'm not mean and cruel and dirty."

There was some precedent for how Richard Williams had raised his daughters in this regard. After all, being African-American, the Williamses were always in a nearly total minority in the tennis world. Two former African-American pros, Rodney Harmon and Bryan Shelton, were on the tour in the 1980s and the early 1990s (in Shelton's case). They, too, felt racial hostility as black tennis players. Both men said that by the time they reached the pro tour they were accustomed to hearing racial barbs. Shelton recalled hearing "comments" toward both him and his mother when he played tournaments in the South. Harmon heard similar things while growing up and playing in Richmond, Virginia. But he said there was a coolness between many pros on the tour.

"Is there racism in tennis? People naturally gravitate to someone who is like them," Harmon said. "Someone who is different definitely is an outsider. Unfortunately, with minorities — because the numbers are not as big — someone can feel alienated. I don't think there is out-and-out racism. But things can happen that are insensitive to minorities. Sometimes that's more a case of neglect and being insensitive than racism."

Shelton put it this way. "When I first started out on the Tour I found it difficult to get practice partners. I felt like I was on my own a little bit. I'm not sure if every player feels that way when you first start out and are trying to get people's respect. I always gave people the benefit of the doubt. I do know for certain I was helped along by some of the black players out there. People like Zina Garrison and Lori McNeil, they took me under their wing and said, 'You're not alone.'"

Martina Hingis, who was already one of the top players of the WTA Tour even though she was a year younger than Venus, said some problems come just because you're a newcomer. "I think it's always hard when you're a newcomer on the Tour," Hingis said. "It wasn't very easy for me, too. The other players just look at you. They don't know what to expect from you because everyone is talking about you, the media pay so much attention. If you don't bring the results, everyone is kind of not very happy because you haven't shown anything to the other players."

Rodney Harmon, asked to comment about the Williams sisters not being very friendly, said, "It kind of frustrates me when people say the Williams sisters aren't friendly. Man, you're playing for money. . . . I had friends on the Tour. But I wasn't *looking* for my best friend to come from the Tour."

So the early attitudes Venus and Serena had seem to have been the result of a combination of factors. They were different, they were African-American, and they hadn't had much contact with other Tour players. They didn't know what to expect, and others didn't know what to expect from them. Because they had each other, as well as their mother and father, they tended to look inward, to each other. Only time would tell whether things would change.

For most of the 1997 season neither sister met with much success. Besides having to adjust to the Tour, they also had to adjust to the different playing surfaces. Most tennis today is played on hard courts. On hard courts, the ball moves at a good pace, and the players get used to the rhythm. In Europe, however, there are still many clay courts. Clay is the slowest of all the playing surfaces. Players must adjust to the slower speeds and learn how to slide when they make quick stops.

There is also grass, which was once the most popular surface in the United States but now exists mainly in England. Grass is the fastest of all tennis surfaces. The best grass players are those who serve and volley and come to the net behind a big serve. On hard courts, players come to the net fewer times, and on clay they rarely come at all. So there are different styles on different surfaces. Some players excel on one surface and are not as good on others. The best players can win on all surfaces, even if they prefer one to the others.

Of the tournaments played on the Tour, there are four that are special. These are the Grand Slam championships. The Grand Slam tournaments are the Australian Open championship; the French Open championship; the all-England championship, better known as Wimbledon; and the U.S. Open championship. The Australian and U.S. championships used to be played on grass. Now they are played on hard courts. The French Open is played on clay. Wimbledon remains the last Grand Slam event played on grass.

In May 1997, Venus played in her first French Open and lost in the opening round. In June, it was on to Wimbledon where she would switch from clay to grass. She had to wait five days for her first match while rain filled the courts. When she finally got to play, it was against an unknown player from Poland, Magdelena Grzybowkska. Venus did not look comfortable on the grass. She served ten double faults, made numerous unforced errors, and lost the match, 4–6, 6–2, 6–4.

Serena couldn't play in the majors yet, as she wouldn't be sixteen until September. Finally, it was time for the U.S. Open. Until then, Venus had not lived up to expectations or her father's predictions. Still playing a limited tournament schedule, she had a 10–9 record in matches played during the season. During the second half of the 1997 season, she wasn't even considered among the top teenagers on the Tour. She came into her country's biggest tournament having failed to reach one final all year.

At the age of sixteen, Martina Hingis was ranked number one in the world and had already won two Grand Slam championships in 1997, the Australian and Wimbledon. There were those who thought Russia's Anna Kournikova would be the next outstanding teen, beating the Williams sisters to the punch. Then there was fifteen-year-old Mirjana Lucic of Croatia, a player Hingis said was "even better than Kournikova and Williams."

Venus was still at the back of the pack, and Serena had not yet been noticed at all. Neither had made much of a name for themselves. Those who had listened to Richard Williams's predictions were quick to point out that most of what he had said about his daughters hadn't happened. The experts felt the U.S. Open would be similar to the French and Wimbledon — another early exit from a major for Venus. After all, it was her first U.S. Open, and that would mean even more pressure on her.

That's when something totally unexpected began happening. Venus started to win. Hitting blistering ground strokes and crushing serves that were approaching 120 miles per hour, she won early round matches against Larisa Neiland and Gala Leon Garcia. It was before her match with

Leon Garcia that Venus's mother said she noticed a change. In practice, Venus was taking some speed off her serve and ground strokes and was starting to mix her shots.

"Something in her head finally clicked," Brandi Williams said. "How not to rush, how to play the game. [It was] just like it clicked with Hingis last year."

In the third round everyone thought it would end. Venus had to go up against the number-eight seed in the tournament, Anke Huber of Germany. However, the girl with a booming serve and beaded hair fooled everyone. Venus showed her whole game — her serve, her speed, her powerful ground strokes — and defeated Huber in a huge upset. Now everyone was taking notice. After showing virtually nothing all year, the seventeen-year-old was playing as she had never played before in one of the world's biggest tournaments.

When she reached the semifinals, she was already the biggest story of the Open. But both the best and the worst were yet to come. In the semis, Venus had to face eleventh-seeded Irina Spirlea of Romania. It was a tough, hard-fought match. At the end of one of the games, as the players walked to their chairs before changing sides, Spirlea bumped into Venus, who pushed her away. It was apparent that there was bad blood between the two. The match finally came down to a third-set tiebreaker. Showing grit and determination, Venus fought off two match points and went on to win.

She had done it. She had played her way into

31

the finals of the U.S. Open at the age of seventeen. But after the match, there was more talk about the bumping incident than the victory. Richard Williams immediately called Spirlea's bump "racially motivated."

Spirlea admitted the bump was intentional, making a remark that indicated she thought Venus was too full of herself. Other players then chipped in about Venus, saying that she had an unfriendly demeanor and talked too much trash.

Lindsay Davenport, who had previously spoken about Venus being unfriendly, said the controversy stemmed more from attitude than from race. "I don't feel it's a problem of race," she explained. "I feel like [Venus has] separated herself from us for whatever reason. . . . Some people have tried [with Venus], but you can only try so much."

When someone compared Venus to Tiger Woods, the young multiracial golfer who was also touted as the next great player in his sport, she said, "I hope [to be like Tiger Woods]," quickly adding, "he's different from the mainstream, and in tennis I also am. I'm tall. I'm black. Everything's different about me. Just face the facts."

The controversy that had started with the Spirlea incident somewhat overshadowed what Venus had accomplished on the court. By winning her semifinals match, she had achieved several important firsts. She was the first woman to reach the finals in her debut U.S. Open since Pam Shriver in 1978. She was also the first unseeded woman to reach the finals since 1958, and the first African-

American woman to reach the finals since Althea Gibson in 1958. Now she would have to meet top-ranked Martina Hingis. The match between seventeen-year-old Venus and sixteen-year-old Hingis was the youngest Grand Slam final in the history of the Open.

Unfortunately, Venus got off to a bad start. Being on center court in the finals of her first Open obviously unnerved her. Hingis romped through the first set without losing a game, winning 6–0. In the second set, Venus began to get into the match. She fought hard but finally dropped the set and the match, 6–4. Still, her run to reach the finals had been truly amazing. She would emerge from the Open as the twenty-seventh-ranked woman in the world.

Hingis, the champion, admitted that Venus had come on strong at the end, but then showed a touch of her own self-confidence when she added, "For the first time [Venus] showed that she can play great. I couldn't know she was going to play that well. But I didn't have many problems today. She plays the game I like. She tried to keep the ball in play. That's too dangerous if you play me."

Even though Venus had made it to the finals, she still hadn't won a Grand Slam. But one of the worst parts of the day was the postmatch press conference. Most of the reporters pressed the issue of racism, asking Venus to respond to comments made by her father about the Spirlea incident. It was difficult for Venus, a teenager, to be asked to comment on very sensitive issues. She finally changed the subject to talk about the fact that the Open was now being played in a brand-new stadium for the first time, a stadium named after the late, great African-American player, Arthur Ashe.

Said Venus, "I think with this moment in the first year in Arthur Ashe Stadium, it all represents everyone being together, everyone having a chance to play. So I think this is definitely ruining the mood, these questions about racism."

It was a very sophisticated way of handling a delicate situation and may have been a turning point. Only time would tell. But one thing was certain. Venus had finally arrived. She had showed the world what a Williams could do. From this point on, the tennis world would be watching Venus Williams. Could sister Serena be far behind?

5
And Then There Were Two

Serena Williams first appeared on the WTA Tour rankings on October 20, 1997, a little more than a month after her sister made it to the finals of the U.S. Open. She was ranked number 453 in the world, a long way from the top. Shortly afterward, she was entered in the Ameritech-sponsored tournament in Chicago. It was just her second WTA Tour main draw event and only the fifth professional tournament of her career. By then, her ranking had improved to 304. Still, no one expected much.

That's when Serena took a page out of Venus's book. She won her first-round match, then surprised everyone by defeating seventh-ranked Mary Pierce in the third round. Like her sister, Serena used a big serve, powerful ground strokes, great speed, and athleticism to wear down her opponent. Was it a fluke? She would find out quickly. Waiting in the quarterfinals was fourth-ranked

Monica Seles, who was already one of the greatest players of all time.

Besides having great talent, Seles was a fighter who never quit. Yet she, too, wilted under the relentless pressure applied by Serena Williams. Serena won. In doing so, she became the lowest-ranked player ever to defeat two top-ten players in one tournament. Another first for the Williams family. Alhough Serena lost in the semifinals, her ranking jumped to 102.

When the 1997 season ended, Venus was the twenty-second-ranked woman in the world, while Serena had moved up to ninety-nine. The tennis world now had two Williamses to contend with. How powerful they would become, no one could know. Before the next year ended, however, more and more people in the tennis world would begin to realize that Richard and Brandi Williams had done something right, something very right. The teenage sisters, who had been groomed to excel, were about to make all those wild predictions come true.

The first Grand Slam event of the season comes early. It's always the Australian Open, which takes place in late January. While their father stayed at home, Brandi accompanied her two girls on the long trip. It took fourteen hours to fly from Florida to Los Angeles, then Los Angeles to Sydney, Australia.

There was a warm-up tournament before the Open, the Adidas International, which was held in Sydney. Venus still didn't have enough computer points to be ranked in the Adidas tournament, and

Serena had to play a qualifying match. With only fifteen matches as a pro, she wasn't automatically in the draw. But she won her qualifying match easily to join her sister in the tournament.

Venus won her first match before having to face top-ranked Martina Hingis in the second round. Hingis had received a bye in the first round, so this was her first match of the season. Venus quickly proved she had learned something in her loss to Hingis at the U.S. Open final the year before. After losing the first set, 3–6, she used her power game to polish off Hingis in the next two sets, 6–4, 7–5, to win the match. It was the first time a number-one-ranked player had lost her first match of the season since computer rankings began in 1975. Once again, a Williams sister was part of a first.

But Venus still had some things to learn. In the final set against Hingis, she was bothered by leg cramps and almost had to stop playing. It was very hot on the court, and her mother had reminded her to drink water. "She just didn't do it," Brandi Williams said, "but from now on she will."

After watching her sister defeat Hingis, Serena also pulled off a shocker in her first match. Playing her own brand of power tennis, she topped second-seed Lindsay Davenport. The Williams sisters had started their 1998 season by defeating the top two women players in the world. They served notice that they would no longer be easy marks for anyone. From there, they continued into the semifinals, and people began talking about the possibility of an all-Williams final. The sisters had never faced each other in a WTA tournament before.

But it wouldn't happen this time. Serena lost her semifinals match to Arantxa Sanchez-Vicario of Spain. Venus made it to the finals, her second. Then she, too, lost to Sanchez-Vicario. Both sisters had been too anxious and made numerous unforced errors when they tried to hit crisp passing shots that Sanchez-Vicario couldn't return.

Now it was time for the Australian Open. Once again there was anticipation before the tournament even began. The way the draw was set up, if both Serena and Venus won their first-round matches, they would have to play each other in the second round. That's exactly what happened. Venus defeated Alexia Dechaume-Balleret, and Serena upset Irina Spirlea, who had had the infamous bumping incident with Venus at the U.S. Open. Now the stage was set.

Venus and Serena would be the first African-American sisters to play against each other in a pro event. It wouldn't be easy for either of them. The realities of the game told them this would happen, so they had prepared. Both being ultimate competitors who hated to lose, they knew they would have to give one hundred percent. They would have to treat each other as just another opponent, an opponent to be beaten.

When it was over, the older sister prevailed. Venus had a little too much power for her sister. The first set was a real struggle, going to a tiebreaker. Venus won it to take the set, 7–6, then waltzed through the second set, 6–1. When the historic match had ended, the two sisters shook hands, then hugged each other. Finally, they turned to the crowd, and with hands held tightly together, they bowed to the cheering Australian fans. Despite all the criticism of the past, the sisters had taken the first step toward winning the respect and admiration of tennis fans.

After the match, Venus had mixed feelings. "It wasn't fun eliminating my sister, but I have to be tough," she said. "After the match, I told her, 'I'm sorry I had to take you out.' Since I am older, I have the feeling I should win. I really wouldn't want to lose. But that's the only person I would be happy losing to because I would say, 'Go ahead, Serena. Go ahead, take the title.'"

Then Venus complimented her younger sister. "Serena's a great player," she said. "She hasn't played that much, and she's taken out people left and right. I had to go out there and be serious because she knows my game. Serena hates to lose, and her reputation is she doesn't lose to anyone twice, so I'm going to be practicing secretly if I want to win the next one."

After losing, the competitive Serena also held her head up. "If I had to lose in the second round," she said, "there's no one better to lose to than Venus."

Venus made it to the quarterfinals before losing to second-seed Lindsay Davenport. But she did emerge from the Australian tournament with her first Grand Slam championship. She teamed with

American Justin Gimelstob to upset the field and win the mixed doubles championship. The win wasn't as prestigious as a singles title, but it was still a big victory. By the time Venus left Australia, she had risen to number fourteen in the world rankings.

Back in the United States, the sisters continued to impress. As expected, it wasn't long before Venus won her first championship. She took the WTA event at Oklahoma City, defeating top-seed Lindsay Davenport in the semis and the fourth seed, Joannette Kruger, in the finals. In that same tournament, she and Serena teamed up to win their first doubles championship.

At the Lipton championships in March, Venus won her second title. As usual, she defeated a number of big names, including Hingis in the semifinals and Anna Kournikova in the finals. The victory moved her into the top-ten rankings for the first time; she was now in the tenth spot. Incredibly, she had jumped one hundred spots from her ranking a year earlier.

Sister Serena also played well at the Lipton, reaching the quarterfinals. She beat three top-thirty players, then had two match points against Hingis in the quarterfinals before faltering and losing the match in a third-set tiebreaker. Serena had moved up to number forty in the rankings. The sisters seemed to be on a determined march to the top. Their athleticism and power game were impressing more people each week. Some long-time observers began to feel that these two girls, if

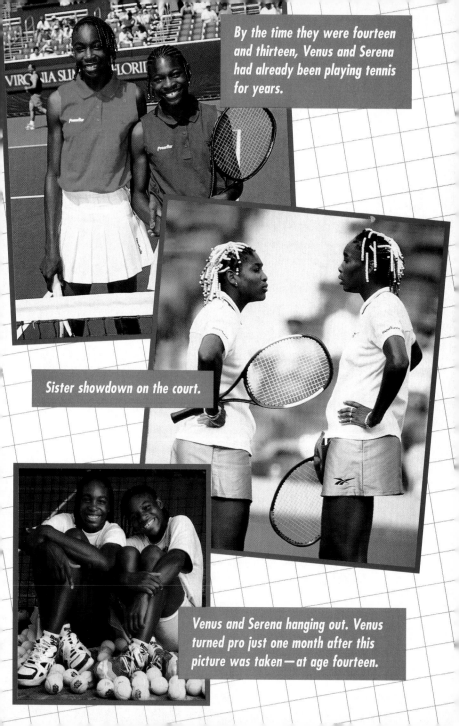

By the time they were fourteen and thirteen, Venus and Serena had already been playing tennis for years.

Sister showdown on the court.

Venus and Serena hanging out. Venus turned pro just one month after this picture was taken—at age fourteen.

At age fourteen, Venus already showed signs of greatness. . . .

Six years later, she is a legend on the court.

At age thirteen, Serena was already a tennis star. . . .

Today, nothing can stop her.

Venus's and Serena's biggest fans: Mom and Dad, Brandi and Richard Williams. Their father is also their manager and coach.

Posing with the Backstreet Boys at Arthur Ashe Kids Day in New York City.

Venus focuses on her serve at the 2000 French Open.

Serena celebrates a point at Wimbledon 2000.

Venus and Serena take time to relax in Monaco.

The Williams sisters get glammed up for the Teen Choice Awards in California.

Serena clutches her first Grand Slam singles championship trophy at the 1999 U.S. Open.

Venus is thrilled about her singles victory at Wimbledon 2000.

Sisterly competition—the Williams sisters meet at the net after Venus beat Serena in the Semifinals at Wimbledon 2000. Venus went on to win her first Grand Slam singles championship in the Finals.

Sharing a laugh after winning a doubles match at Wimbledon 2000.

Serena and Venus wave to their fans as they celebrate their victory in the doubles championship at Wimbledon 2000.

they stayed healthy and continued to improve, had a good chance to someday be numbers one and two in the world, and perhaps rank among the best ever.

After the Lipton tournament, Richard Williams made an interesting observation. After losing to Venus in the semifinals, Martina Hingis complained of being tired. That was odd since she hadn't played the day before meeting Venus and had skipped the tournament the week before. Mr. Williams saw the fatigue as something else.

"The pressure of being number one has drained . . . Hingis," he said. "I've told Venus that 1998 is her year to take the number-one spot. But, as sad as this sounds, I kind of hope she doesn't take it this year. These girls, when they become number one, they look older, they act older, they get tired fast. It's the pressure."

There was pressure on the Tour, and the number-one player was always a target. Yet Venus seemed to sense that she had something going for her that most of the other players did not. In speaking about Hingis, Venus said, "She isn't as strong as I am. A lot of times the strong person doesn't have to think as much as the next person. When I learn to [think more], I'm going to become a much better player."

One of the most qualified judges of Venus's talents was Andre Agassi, who was often in the fight for number one among the men. Knowing the game as well as anyone, Agassi saw the tremendous attributes that Venus brought to her sport. "I think she's the best athlete the women's game has seen so far," he said. "Now it's a matter of how she puts it all together. She's going to beat ninety-nine percent of the girls because of the athlete she is."

Both sisters continued to impress. Heading back to Europe in preparation for the French Open, Venus made a Tour stop at Zurich, where she met Mary Pierce in the quarterfinals. On match point, she unleashed an incredible serve that Pierce couldn't touch. The speed gun made everyone in the crowd look twice. Venus's serve was clocked at 127.4 miles per hour, the fastest serve ever recorded in WTA Tour history. She didn't win the tournament, but her booming serve was the talk of the tennis world.

The Italian Open was a clay-court event that gave everyone a chance to prepare for the upcoming French Open. It always took some time to adjust to the slower surface. Venus had played on clay before, but it was Serena's first tournament on that surface. That was hard to tell from the early rounds, however. Serena upset twelfth-ranked Nathalie Tauziat of France in her first match; then beat number twenty-one Joannette Kruger; and four-time champion, the eighth-ranked Conchita Martinez of Spain to reach the quarterfinals. Guess who was waiting to play her there? That's right. Sister Venus.

So the two met again, and for the second time, big sister won. Both knew, however, that Serena's turn would come sooner or later. Venus went on to defeat Sanchez-Vicario in the semifinals before losing to Hingis in a three-set final match. The loss ended her eleven-match win streak and once again showed the fierce rivalry that was developing between the two teenage stars.

Then came the French Open. Serena won early, then topped fifteenth-seeded Dominique Van Roost to reach the fourth round of the tournament. There she had to meet Arantxa Sanchez-Vicario, who was often at her best on clay. It turned out to be a good match but ended in controversy, with a Williams sister right in the middle.

In the first set, Serena looked as if she was going to overpower her opponent. She stood inside the baseline to take Sanchez-Vicario's first serves early, and she slammed backhand winners. Besides her expected power, Serena also added a few well-placed drop shots and a beautiful lob over her opponent's head. Then, late in the set, the controversy began.

Serena hit a winner past Sanchez-Vicario, then seemed to glare at her for a moment. Was it intended to intimidate? Perhaps. Was it gamesmanship? Perhaps. On the next point, she slammed another winner after her opponent slipped on the court. Sanchez-Vicario began arguing with the referee, claiming the ball had bounced twice before Serena hit it. Suddenly, the two players were at the net, talking heatedly to each other.

"I said to her, 'Arantxa, Arantxa, one bounce, one bounce,'" Serena said.

Sanchez-Vicario, however, said she didn't like the way Serena had talked. "She came to the net talking very aggressively," Arantxa said. "I don't think she can act that way. I don't think it's nice at all."

On the next point, Serena won the first set, 6–4, and Sanchez-Vicario slammed her racket to the court.

"Every time I see her play a match, she always argues about almost every call," Serena said. "If she didn't do that, then I would have been a little surprised because she argues a lot."

Then came the second set. Serena took a 3–2 lead. Then Sanchez-Vicario asked for a time-out to change her outfit. She left the court for three minutes and changed from a black outfit to a white one, claiming she needed the change because her outfit was sweaty and uncomfortable. Serena didn't feel that was the truth. She felt the change was more of a psychological tactic.

"I think she thought the white dress would be a better tactic against me," she said.

After taking a 5–2 lead in the second set and being on the brink of taking the match, Serena's game collapsed. Sanchez-Vicario rallied to win the set, 7–5, then went on to take the third, 6–3, to win the match. Serena had made too many unforced errors and seemed to lose confidence. In the seventh game of the final set, Sanchez-Vicario accused Serena of hitting a ball at her head as the two rallied close to the net.

"She went to hit me," said Sanchez-Vicario. "I was lucky that I went to the other side. It just passed me. She just started laughing, looking at me badly. I just think she doesn't have respect. She cannot go in with that attitude. You know, I'm glad that I beat her. That's the thing — I taught her a lesson."

After it was over, Serena did not want to say any more. The bottom line was that she lost. "I'm only sixteen, my first [French Open]," she said. "Everything is a learning experience for me."

Venus didn't do much better in singles, losing in the quarterfinals. But the sisters still had some excitement for the French crowd. Both reached the finals of the mixed doubles, where Venus and Justin Gimelstob defeated Serena and Luis Lobo, 6–4, 6–4. It was the second straight Grand Slam mixed doubles title for Venus and Gimelstob, and the first finals appearance for Serena. The sisters didn't play women's doubles together because they felt they didn't have enough experience to play together on clay.

From the French Open, the players quickly move on to grass to prepare for Wimbledon, which is held the very next month. One of the warm-up tournaments is held at Eastbourne, England, and both sisters were entered. This one would be another first, but not one that Venus wanted to remember. Playing a first-round match on June 17, her eighteenth birthday, Venus was beaten very easily by Natasha Zvereva. The score was 6–2, 6–1. Zvereva was known more as a doubles specialist, and no one had expected her to win.

"I was very inconsistent and didn't play well," Venus said. "I didn't serve well at all. I've learned that I'm going to have to practice harder and be more serious in my practices. I wasn't overconfi-dent, but in practice I should play every point as if I were in a match. Sometimes when I practice, I try a lot of different things instead of really focus-ing." Venus had learned something very impor-tant. Those lessons always stuck. Neither of the sisters consistently make the same mistake twice.

Serena played into the quarterfinals at that tour-nament, where she once again lost to Sanchez-Vicario. But it was the first tournament in which Serena advanced further than her big sister. She was now ranked twentieth in the world, with Venus in the number-six slot. They were moving up the rankings quickly and easily. Opponents had to contend with two power players with beaded braids and booming serves. Venus and Serena were beginning to strike fear into the rest of the tour. Now both were looking forward to Wimble-don, where one of them hoped to take their first singles Grand Slam championship.

6
Old-Fashioned Hard Work

Venus was the sixth-seeded woman at the 1998 Wimbledon tournament. Serena, playing there for the first time, was unseeded. Although both girls were still in their teens, they were now star attractions wherever they went. They certainly stood out. Their trademark beaded hair, powerful physical appearance, and booming serves were unmistakable.

Venus had once said she was different because she was tall and black. The real difference, however, was the way she and her sister played the game. When they were playing well, they could overpower many of the other players on the Tour. Only the top women with superior skills could compete with them. Yet at nearly seventeen and at eighteen, the question was how much better they could become. Both girls seemed ready to work as hard as they could to reach the top. Their father continued to predict they would become the two top players in the world. Venus and Serena indicated that was their goal as well.

"I'm definitely ready to win," Venus said when asked of her expectations at Wimbledon.

Serena, however, made an interesting analysis of her sister's game. "Some days Venus can be a force, and others she can be a completely different person," the younger Williams said. "I eradicated that tendency a long time ago. I concentrate properly on the surface involved, which is something Venus is struggling to do."

Serena was talking about her sister's surprise defeat at Eastbourne a short time earlier, when she appeared unsure and ill at ease on the grass courts. Consistency is often the last quality a champion acquires. If what Serena said was true, Venus had a lot of work to do. So did Serena. She was still playing in her first real year on the circuit. Each tournament was still an adventure. Wimbledon, as it turned out, would be a big disappointment for both of them.

Serena won her first two matches, including a second-round victory over fellow teenager Mirjana Lucic. But during her third-round match, a leg injury forced her to retire, ending her singles run. Venus reached the quarterfinals but was then beaten by Czech veteran Jana Novotna in a close match, 7–5, 7–6. Novotna would go on to win the championship. The only consolation was Serena returning from her injury and winning the mixed doubles title with partner Max Mirnyi.

After Wimbledon, the girls played on. Venus was bothered during the summer months by tendinitis in her knee and missed several tournaments. She won a third title, the 1998 Grand Slam

Cup, defeating Sanchez-Vicario, Nathalie Tauziat, and Patty Schnyder along the way. Serena, though now hovering around the top twenty in rankings, had still not won a singles title. The very great players are almost always judged on the number of Grand Slam singles titles they win, and neither sister had won a Slam.

They would try once again at the 1998 U.S. Open. Before the tournament even started, Richard Williams said he was more concerned with his daughters' educations than their tennis careers. Then he made a statement that surprised many. "You know what I wish? I wish they'd quit tennis and move on to other things," he said. "Tennis is a good way to make a million dollars, but they've done that already, and then some. They're so brilliant, they'll be great in anything they do. And people won't be asking me if I'm going to be sitting in some stadium watching them play."

Mr. Williams then talked about the continuing education of the girls, even while they rose in the tennis rankings. He also reminded everyone that he and his wife made sure that academics were not forgotten.

"Tennis is something to do for a few years," he said, "but I'm more interested in what they do with the rest of their lives. They're learning computers, and they know that comes first. Last year, it wasn't sure that Venus would play in the U.S. Open until four days before when her computer grades got up to where they should be. This summer, Serena canceled out of a tournament because she was getting an A minus in her computer

49

course instead of the A plus she knows she has to get."

Mr. Williams might have had a habit of exaggerating a bit when he talked about his daughters, but he did make sure that the girls were always taking courses, always learning, always broadening the scope of their knowledge. He was also telling the truth when he talked about their earnings. They still hadn't won a fortune in prize money, but both already had endorsement deals worth several million dollars for shoes and clothing. If they started winning major tournaments, it was apparent that tennis could make both of them — as well as the entire family — very wealthy.

The U.S. Open followed the pattern that had been established at previous Grand Slam events. Venus advanced further than Serena in singles, but not far enough. Serena played well in the opening two rounds, then in round three had to meet Irina Spirlea. The year before, of course, Spirlea and Venus had their "bumping" incident. Reporters tried to make it into some kind of grudge match, but Spirlea quickly dispelled that. "We shake hands already," she said. "We talked. . . . It is normal with them, and they are normal with everybody else, you know, everybody is happy."

It was a strange match. Spirlea won the first set, 6–3. Then Serena took over. In the second set she was all over the court, showing the crowd her incredible athleticism. She saved points with acrobatic lunges, slammed sizzling passing shots from both sides, and looked as if she simply couldn't lose. She won the second set in a 6–0 blitz.

"I know that she is going to get to every point," Spirlea said afterward. "But inside of you, you think it is finished. You say, 'I won,' and then you see the ball coming and it's, like, 'Oh, no, it is coming back!'"

In the third set, Serena lost some of the edge. Her serve was spotty, and she had trouble holding in several games. Spirlea finally broke her in the eleventh game of the set, then served out the match to win, 7–5. It was a huge disappointment. But Serena had offered everyone a glimpse of her all-court, overall game. If she got it all under control, watch out!

As for Venus, she played well and made it to the semifinals once again. It looked as if she had a good chance to win. But she came up short. This time she lost to Lindsay Davenport, who would go on to take the title. The score was 6–4, 6–4. Davenport played a power game, but Venus, obviously, wasn't very far behind. It had been a breakthrough year for her. At the end of the season she would be ranked number five in the world. But she still hadn't won a Grand Slam.

One tradition continued at that year's Open. Serena and Max Mirnyi of Belarus won the mixed doubles title. Venus and Justin Gimelstob had won the Australian and French mixed doubles. Now Serena and Mirnyi had won Wimbledon and the U.S. Open. When the year ended, Serena would be ranked twentieth in the world after just one full year on the Tour.

Things on the Tour had gotten better in many ways for the Williams sisters. Now that the other players were getting to know them, there were fewer claims of unfriendliness and aloofness. Venus and Serena came from a different world from that of many of the other women. They had a style of their own and each other for support. After all, no other players had a sister along with them most of the time. That the sisters should hang together shouldn't really have been much of a surprise.

Some people already saw the Williams sisters as special. After the Open, Rick Reilly, writing in *Sports Illustrated*, said about Venus and Serena, "The Williams sisters are cocky and insular. They're also gorgeous, rich, smart, polite, gifted, well-spoken, huge and improving like mad. . . . How many millionaire sisters have only one friend — each other? How many can say they speak French and are learning Russian and Portuguese? How many sit down at a press conference and challenge reporters to look up the derivation of words?

"I admire the way they're unafraid of tennis's virtually all-white press, tennis's virtually all-white locker rooms and, come to think of it, virtually all-white tennis. They say what they want, say it well and hate to lose . . . the truth is, the Williams family is the best thing to happen to women's tennis since the scrunchee."

Because tennis players travel the world and because there are so many foreign players in the game, the girls were learning different languages. They were learning about business, about computers, and Venus was beginning to show interest in fashion design.

At the beginning of the 1999 season they were a bit older, more mature, and even more physically imposing. With her long arms and long legs, Venus looked as if she could reach everything that came her way. Her serves were consistently more than a hundred miles per hour, and she was always capable of booming one in the 125-mile-per-hour range. Serena was shorter but more muscular. She, too, could boom serves past the hundred-mile-per-hour mark. Her court coverage sometimes defied description, and she always fought like a tiger until the very end. Some said she hated to lose even more than Venus did.

The family decided on a different strategy in 1999. The sisters would not play in the same tournament unless it was absolutely necessary. That way, they could avoid playing against each other as much as possible. Although they knew it would sometimes be inevitable, the sisters really didn't like playing against each other. Both were naturally competitive and didn't want to lose, but there was no joy in beating each other. They were so close that they shared each other's joy at winning and suffered with each other when one lost. So if they played each other, the outcome could only be met with mixed emotions.

The new strategy gave the sisters an opportunity to make history once again. It happened the final week of February. Venus was defending her title in the IGA SuperThrift Tennis Classic, held in Oklahoma City. Meanwhile, Serena was in Paris, playing in the Gaz de France Open. Both sisters battled their way into the respective finals. Because of the difference in time zones, Serena's final came first.

Playing against French teen Amélie Mauresmo, Serena had to fight for consistency. She won the first set, 6–2, dropped the second, 3–6, and finally prevailed in a tiebreaker, winning it 7–4, which gave her the third set and the match by a 7–6 count. It was her first ever singles title.

Back in Oklahoma, Venus was preparing for her finals against Amanda Coetzer when she received the news about her sister. "When I found out she had won I really felt that it was my duty to come out here and win," she said.

Venus wasted little time. She broke Coetzer in the first game, then the two stayed on serve until Venus won the set, 6–4. In the second set, Venus turned it up a notch and blitzed Coetzer in just twenty-one minutes by a 6–0 count. She had ten aces in the day and completed the tournament without losing a single set. With her victory, she and Serena became the first sisters ever to win WTA Tour events on the same day.

All week the two had encouraged each other by sending e-mail messages back and forth on their computers. Even though they were a continent apart with an ocean between them, the two sisters remained in constant touch. After their victories, they met at Indian Wells, California, for the tournament in which the winner would receive the Evert Cup, named after women's tennis great Chris Evert.

Venus would be a spectator, sitting in the stands with her father. Serena had a tough road to the finals. Still unseeded, she had to meet top-ten players Lindsay Davenport and Mary Pierce in the quarters and semis, but she topped both. In the finals, she would have to play Germany's Steffi Graf, one of the greatest women champions ever.

Serena came out playing her usual power game. In the first set, she seemed to have too much for the twenty-nine-year-old veteran and won the set, 6–3. Then, in the second, Graf called on her years of experience and countered Serena's sizzling ground strokes and powerful serves with a variety of spins, lobs, and passing shots. The strategy worked. Serena was taken out of her rhythm, and Graf won the set, 6–3, to even the match.

For the first six games of the final set it looked like more of the same. Graf broke Serena early and after six games held a 4–2 lead. All Graf had to do was hold serve and she would win the match. After Serena held her own serve to make it 4–3, she regrouped, let her talent take over, and broke Graf's serve. That evened the match at 4–4. Both held in the next two games to make it 5–5. Serena then took over once again, easily holding her own serve, then breaking Graf to win the set and the match, 7–5.

"It means a lot to me because Steffi is a great champion," Serena said after her win. "She has more titles than any man or lady [now active] in tennis. It's very exciting for me. I'm only seventeen and I have a lot to look forward to. This is the biggest tournament I've ever won. I know I can win the big ones now."

And of course, it was another first for the Williams sisters. Going into the tournament, Serena was ranked twenty-first. That made her the lowest-ranked player ever to win a Tier I event since the tier structure began in 1980. After the tournament, her ranking jumped up to number seventeen.

Now both sisters were off to Florida to compete in the Lipton championships. Venus was the defending champion, but Serena was also entered. There was extra special fan interest because the two were playing in the same tournament. Fans seemed to want to see the two sisters go up against each other. The girls were placed in separate halves of the draw. If they met, it could only happen in the final. Venus was seeded sixth in the tournament, Serena sixteenth.

Even though they seemed to be making an easy march to the top, the sisters weren't letting tennis be their only priority. Before the Lipton, it was announced that the two young stars were launching a monthly newsletter called *Tennis Monthly Recap*. It was said they did it to diversify themselves a bit and also to combat a Tour schedule that could get boring.

Serena had talked about becoming a journalist someday, and kidded by saying she might have to interview herself for the next issue, because "It's a hot story." Other players quickly showed their respect for their new endeavor. The men's top-ranked player, Pete Sampras, had turned down many interview requests while playing at Indian Wells. Yet he agreed to allow Venus and Serena to interview him for their Wimbledon issue.

Although they were stretching their wings in other directions, tennis obviously continued to be a top priority. In the early rounds of the Lipton, both sisters seemed to be in top form. Serena had convincing wins over Monica Seles and Amanda Coetzer. Now she was ready to meet top-ranked Martina Hingis in the semifinals.

Anytime either of the Williams sisters meets Martina Hingis, it's a battle. In the match between Serena and Hingis that was supposed to be power against finesse, it turned out to be flow and ebb, each player going on streaks while the other made too many unforced errors. Hingis raced off to a 4–0 lead in the first set only to have Serena catch fire to win the next six and take the set, 6–4. Serena continued to show the way, winning the first two games of the second set.

Then it was Hingis's turn again. She won the next five games for a 5–2 lead and appeared on the brink of evening the match. That's when Serena once again showed the kind of fighter she is. She seized the momentum from Hingis and began to rally. With Hingis leading, 6–5, and serving for the set, Serena jumped all over the Hingis serve, ripped several winners, and broke serve to tie the match at 6-all. In the tiebreaker, she hit three straight forehand winners, then slammed yet another to win the tiebreaker, 7–3, and the match.

It was Serena's sixteenth straight victory. "I've worked really hard all my life since I was four years old," Serena said, afterward. "There comes a time when you have to start winning. All my hard work is finally paying off. I guess it's my biggest win. I've never beaten the number-one player before."

In analyzing the difference between Hingis and Serena, one observer noted that Serena's final serve of the match came in at 110 miles per hour. Hingis's final serve, by contrast, was clocked at just 84 miles per hour. That was the kind of physical advantage both Williams sisters had over most of the other women on the tour. Now Serena was in the finals. Would Venus follow?

Venus had had some tough matches in the tournament, including a big win over Jana Novotna in the quarterfinals, the first time she had ever defeated Novotna. But it wouldn't get easier. In her semifinals, Venus had to meet the always tough Steffi Graf.

Against Graf, Venus pretty much had her A game going. She won the first set, 6–2, then cruised in the second, 6–4, to win the match. In both sets she took 3–0 leads, playing powerful but patient tennis and allowing Graf to make mistakes. She also broke her opponent's serve six times. There was about to be yet another first — two sisters meeting in a WTA Tour final.

"Their athleticism is incredible," said Steffi Graf about the Williams sisters. "They move extremely well. They're taking risks. They go for their shots. They don't have a certain weakness. They're very tall and big. That's definitely a plus. All those things are definitely working for them."

Before it started, it was apparent that both sisters wanted to win this match. Serena said, "I've always been in the background. It's time for me to move forward now. I'm playing the best tennis I have in my young career." She apparently didn't want to be the little sister any longer.

As for Venus, she expressed it this way. "I don't like putting my name and losing in the same sentence. Winning and Venus sounds great. Serena doesn't like to lose, either."

Once again the sisters' supreme confidence was apparent. Asked if a new era had arrived in women's tennis, Venus at first said she guessed so. Pressed by the reporter, she finally said, "I could say it, yes. A new era has arrived this week in women's tennis."

Watching the girls practice together the day before the final, Richard Williams said he was extremely proud of both girls. Then he showed he would forever be a father when he said, "My only hope in watching my babies is that I don't cry."

The classic match was played on March 28, 1999, the first all-sister finals in 115 years. Venus had won the sisters' two previous meetings, but Serena was now a better, more confident player. Many thought she would win. Shortly after the match began, an emotional Richard Williams had to leave the stadium briefly. Many things were going through his mind. "I thought about all the problems we've had in tennis, bringing the girls up, how difficult it was, the gang members, all the people out there. I was saying, 'Look where you are today.' It was so difficult for me to believe it."

On the court, however, it was all business. The first set was completely dominated by Venus. Using her speed and long reach, Serena just couldn't seem to get anything past her. Set one went to the older sister, 6–1. In the second set, Serena the fighter came out. With Venus leading 4–3, Serena gritted her teeth and played superbly. She won three straight games to take the set, 6–4. Venus suddenly seemed shaky, making a number of surprising errors.

No one could doubt the competitiveness between the two. When Venus took a 2–1 lead in the third and final set, Serena threw her racket across the court, angry at herself. "After a while you're thinking, 'I can win,'" she said, afterward. "You're not thinking about who you're playing."

Once again, Serena rallied, knotting the set at 4–4. But in the next two games, Serena committed seven unforced errors, allowing Venus to close out the match at 6–4. The older sister had won once again.

Usually when a player wins a tough match there is some kind of celebration, a smile, a pumping fist, maybe both arms raised in victory. Not this time. In fact, the moment the match ended, Venus's shoulders seemed to sag with relief. She walked to the net, showing no sign of happiness or joy. Nor did she gesture toward her parents or crack even the smallest of smiles. She just gave Serena a somber high five, then put her arm around her sister's shoulder, and the two walked off the court together.

"It's not too big," Venus said afterward. "In the end we go home, we live life. You have to be happy after that. You have to remind yourself it's a game, and there's only one winner. Next week there will be another opportunity."

Serena, too, seemed to look at the match as a family affair. "I definitely look forward to another finals with Venus," she said. "It's what we always dreamed of."

Unfortunately, the match didn't end without some controversy. A few people looked at the sudden rash of unforced errors by Venus that allowed Serena to come back and win the second set. There was speculation that she had let up intentionally, that perhaps their father had told the girls to go three sets to make the match more dramatic. The family emphatically denied it.

"I would never tell my daughters to do that," Richard said. "As a matter of fact, I think my daughters should get off that concrete as soon as possible."

Venus also scoffed at the implication. "Serena always comes back and beats people," she said. "I didn't want to become another victim. It was all I could do to hold her off."

The much anticipated finals meeting was history. Now the Grand Slam events were coming up. Venus left the Lipton as the number-six-ranked player in the world. Serena moved up to number eleven. It was Serena who put a final stamp on the tournament and what the historic meeting really meant when she said, "Venus is a great player. I'm a great, awesome player, too."

7
Pointing Toward a Grand Slam

With both sisters playing well, they felt it was time for them to begin winning Grand Slam singles titles. The French Open was coming up, followed by Wimbledon, and finally the U.S. Open. The consensus was that there would be a Williams taking the top prize in one or more of them. At this point, most felt it would probably be Venus.

In late April, about a month before the French Open, the family announced the formation of another charitable endeavor. They had already put money into programs that encourage children to stay in school and avoid drugs. Now Richard Williams said he had invested $700,000 of family funds into forming the Williams & Williams Charter Bus Service in West Palm Beach, Florida. The service would enable tennis fans, for $150 each, to take a three-hour bus ride to a posh resort, have lunch, and hit a few tennis balls with Venus and Serena.

"Every penny we make will go to underprivileged programs," Mr. Williams said. "We expect to do $15,000 to $20,000 per outing. I know it's not much money, but it's a lot of money to those programs."

The sisters had already earned $3 million in prize money since turning pro. That didn't include endorsement deals and bonuses. Their overall income was much higher. Now they were starting to give back.

But in May, it was back to tennis business. First they had to play on the slow clay surface of the French Open. Clay is the most difficult surface for power players like the Williamses. Because the ball moves slower, power players lose some of their effectiveness. Although they were power players, Venus and Serena had developed such fine, all-around games that it was felt that they could, indeed, challenge for the title. In fact, Venus had won the Italian Open on clay just a few weeks before the French. Venus was seeded fifth in the tournament, Serena tenth.

Both won their first two matches to advance to the third round. They looked to be in fine form and both were upbeat. "This is my ninth Grand Slam," Venus said. "Now it's time for me to make a move. I'm ready."

Serena put it this way. "It's just a matter of time before I reach the top spot or reach my goals. I plan on doing well here. But I'm taking one match at a time because in the past, I would look too far ahead in the draw and not do too well."

Unfortunately, the magic didn't last. Serena lost in the third round, Venus in the fourth. It was disappointing to be out of a Grand Slam so early. Being the kind of athletes they were, the sisters regrouped to play together in the doubles. Working together, they fought their way into the finals. Now they would have to meet Martina Hingis and Anna Kournikova in a battle of four teenage tennis sensations. The match was hard fought. When it ended, after two rain delays, the Williams sisters had the title.

"We should have finished it off in two," said Serena, always confident and always feeling she could do better. "We should have just stayed calm and made our shots. We just got too tense and didn't perform."

They performed well enough, however, to take a Grand Slam doubles title. But it was that singles crown that still eluded both of them. Now it was time for the change from clay to grass — Wimbledon. Maybe their power games would bring one of them the championship in England.

Then, on the eve of the tournament, Serena Williams suddenly withdrew, citing a bad case of the flu. WTA officials were upset to lose the number-ten seed. With Venus seeded sixth, there had already been anticipation of the two sisters meeting in the fourth round. Richard Williams was contacted to see if there was any way his daughter could play. He said no.

"She has a terrible case of the flu," Mr. Williams said. "I took her to the doctor this morning, and he told her it was best to rest and take it easy. She's been sick for the last two or three days, but last night she had a bad fever, and the doctor believes it will go on for at least a week. Serena wanted to go to Wimbledon and give it a try . . . but the doctor said again it was better if she rested."

Their father also indicated that Venus had a case of the flu as well, but it wasn't nearly as bad as her sister's. "Venus is a little sluggish because they hang out a lot together," he explained, "but we're hoping she'll be all right."

Venus started out strongly. When she defeated Sarah Pitkowsky, 6–1, 6–1, in the third round, the flu was obviously not holding her back. She was again one of the favorites to win the title. Her fourth-round match was against Russia's Anna Kournikova. Kournikova had talent but had never won a single tournament. Some said she didn't concentrate enough on her game because of the amount of attention she received off the court.

That wasn't a problem for the Williams sisters. They were getting the same kind of attention, but the game came first. Venus polished off Kournikova in three sets, 3–6, 6–3, 6–2. Now it was on to the quarters where she would again meet Steffi Graf. The veteran champion had missed nearly a year after knee surgery but had come back to win the French Open and was playing very well at Wimbledon. Venus knew it wouldn't be an easy match.

There were numerous rain delays, and it took seven hours to complete the three-set encounter. Rain delays can take a player out of her rhythm, change momentum, and even open a player up to injury. In the first set, Venus couldn't win the key points; Graf's forehand, always a potent weapon, was constantly finding the corners of the court for winners. Graf won the first set, 6–2.

Even when they don't win, the Williams sisters rarely go quietly in straight sets. Not surprisingly, Venus came back in a tough second set. At one point, Graf fought off six break points before Venus finally took the game. After yet another rain delay, Venus evened the match, 6–3, to set up a third and decisive set. Once again these two outstanding players slugged it out in an exciting match that had the crowd at the edge of their seats. Another rain delay, this one of nearly two hours, kept everyone guessing about the outcome. Finally, the players returned to do battle once more.

The set was tied at 2–2, with Venus serving, when Graf unleashed two monster forehands to get the first break of the set. An unforced error by Venus helped Graf hold serve in the next game, giving her a 4–2 lead. Both players held serve, bringing the score to 5–3 and leaving Graf just one game from victory. Venus then held serve to make it 5–4. Now she had to break Graf to stay in the match.

At 40–30, it was match point for Graf. Venus returned Graf's serve, but then the veteran German star slammed three booming forehands. Venus returned the first two, but the third went into the net. It was over. A dejected Venus left the court, another Grand Slam opportunity gone.

If it was any consolation, she had lost to a great

champion. Graf, for her part, had nothing but praise for her young opponent. "The match really was at the highest level," she said. "It rarely happens in a quarterfinal that you have to play that sort of tennis. She is very tough, she has a big serve, moves incredibly well, and she got some balls back that I thought were over. Two years ago you could see what potential she has, and I've said it before and I'll say it again, she will be world number one."

Predictions, however, don't mean much when you have just been eliminated from Wimbledon. Venus was disappointed. She felt she was ready for that final step. It hadn't happened this time.

"I played well," she told reporters, "but I could have played better, especially on some key points. It's too late to change anything I've done [today], but I can change the future. For instance, I should have been more aggressive on the break points. I guess I'll just have to work even harder."

After Wimbledon, there were other tournaments and more tough competition. The sisters, like the other players on the Tour, wanted to win every time out. But there was one big thing in the back of their minds — the U.S. Open in September. They had reached a point where they were both winning tournaments and were ranked in the top ten. The one thing that neither sister had yet done was win a Grand Slam singles title. They certainly were confident that they could win. Other people, including their fellow pros, were saying they were good enough to win, good enough to rise to the absolute top of their sport. What remained was for Venus and Serena to go out and prove it — to themselves, their family, and everyone else.

When the seedings for the U.S. Open were announced, Venus was at number three and Serena was seeded seventh. Since the girls were on opposite sides of the draw, there was a chance that they would meet in the final. To further emphasize the sisters' growing popularity and high visibility, a new series of advertisements appeared the week of the Open. Venus and Serena became the latest athletes to appear in the "milk mustache" ads. The ad showed the sisters in their tennis outfits, beaded hair, and two white "milk mustaches" on their upper lips.

It was incredible how far the sisters had come in a short time. When they first joined the Tour many people viewed them with suspicion. They weren't always friendly, seemed confrontational at times, and always had their father nearby. In addition, they were both physically imposing, a quality people sometimes view as threatening.

But as the 1999 U.S. Open got under way, it was apparent how much things had changed. Not only were the girls huge favorites with the crowds, they were also popular among the other players. They had a special quality that created excitement and anticipation whenever they appeared.

Venus and Serena were for real, both as tennis players and human beings. Despite being young, they were thinkers. They did things with a purpose and for a reason. Yet they still knew how to have fun. They had achieved a balance in their life while swimming in the fishbowl of professional athletics.

For several years, foreign journalists had been asking why the sisters were not received better in the United States despite their obvious great talent. Finally, the girls were getting their due. The fans at the U.S. Open roared in delight each time one of the sisters took the court.

There was increasing speculation about the possibility of a Williams–Williams final. Whenever they faced reporters, there were questions about the possibility of the sisters meeting in the final.

"I hope we can do that well," Venus said. "It would be great."

Serena agreed. "Either way, one of us would be able to win our first Grand Slam."

Serena also said that the fact that she was the younger of the two wouldn't mean a thing in determining the outcome of the match. "It has nothing to do with who's younger," Serena said. "It's about who's playing well and who's not."

With Richard Williams continuing to predict that his daughters would be facing each other in the final, the girls continued to advance. In the quarterfinals, Venus topped Anke Huber of Germany, and Serena won over Monica Seles. Now they were just one match away from what could be a historical meeting. Seles, a former champion, seemed to recognize what was coming for everyone over the next few years.

"Now it's Venus and Serena's time," Seles said.

The semifinals wouldn't be easy. Serena would be taking the court first, meeting Lindsay Davenport, the defending champion. Then it would be Venus's turn. She would be meeting arch rival Martina Hingis. In the minds of many, these were the four best women players in the world. The two who would advance to the finals would surely have to earn it.

Serena and Davenport both began slugging the ball early in a battle of power players. Davenport was the one player who could come close to matching the Williams sisters in the power department. But she didn't have their speed. If Serena could exploit this, she could win. With Venus watching, Serena won the first set, 6–4. After the set, Venus left the court to begin preparing for her match. Had she stayed, she wouldn't have liked what she saw. In the next twenty-four minutes, Serena's game fell apart, and Davenport blitzed through the set, winning it, 6–1, to even the match.

"Lindsay was playing just unbelievably," Serena said. "She was hitting shots for winners, just attacking everything. I became really determined. I was, like, 'I'm tired of this. I want something also.'"

So it was on to the third set. Could Serena regain the magic? She was serving first and quickly sent a message to her opponent. She slammed three straight aces past the lunging Davenport and took the first game. The two stayed on serve until the score was 3–3. That's when Serena got the first break. She set it up with a running forehand volley crosscourt. On break point, a little luck entered the picture.

Serena lunged for a return and mishit the ball. Instead of going out of bounds, as most mishits do, this one squirted just over the net. Davenport tried to scoop it, but it was long, and Serena had her service break and a 4–3 lead.

With the match in sight, Serena held serve after fighting off five break points in what was a brilliant game. She finally won it, making the score 5–3. Later, she called it the turning point of the match. "I felt that if I won that game, I would have a great chance of winning the match because all I had to do was hold serve," she said. "I felt if Lindsay won the game, I would have to fight. I was never going to give up. I never at one time felt I was going to lose."

Serena closed out the match with three service winners, then an ace, her fifty-fourth of the tournament, more than any other woman. More important, she had won the match, 6–3, 1–6, 6–4, to advance to her first ever Grand Slam final!

Serena had played a great match. Her relentless battling and incredible power eventually wore down her opponent. The younger Williams sister was proud of the way she had played. "I really think I've developed mentally a lot," she said. "I'm more composed out there. I didn't get nervous or anything. I just stayed determined and focused. I'm able to pull through."

Davenport couldn't say enough about her opponent. "Every break point I had, she just hit a huge,

huge first serve," the defending champion said. "She has a great serve, one of the best in women's tennis, if not the best. She throws in one at 115 miles per hour, then she'll slow it up. She has a great kick serve. She mixes it up better than her sister does. That's what you have to deal with — the serve, getting them back, but still be aggressive. It's a hard thing to do."

So it was one down and one to go. Serena was in the final. If Venus could come out and defeat Martina Hingis, the U.S. Open would have the all-Williams final that Richard Williams and others had predicted. Venus had lost to Hingis in the finals two years earlier but had beaten her numerous times since. Theirs was a classic power versus finesse rivalry. Hingis couldn't match the power of either Williams sister. She was a great champion because of her overall court presence, her great anticipation, and her sense of timing and pace. Her tennis instincts were brilliant, and she always seemed to know what her opponent would do next. That's why she was so hard to beat.

The match was called more a battle of wills than a display of beautiful tennis. Both players produced their share of spectacular shots, and both had trouble holding serve. Before the match ended, Venus would be broken nine times, Hingis six. In the first set, Hingis outplayed Venus. Her shots were brilliant, her placements superb. Even with her great speed and reach, Venus couldn't reach Martina's passing shots. She lost the first set by a decisive 6–1 score.

In the second set, Venus showed the fighter she

was. Playing steadier tennis, she rallied to even the match by a 6–4 count. Like her sister, she had one set to go to reach the finals.

Despite winning the set, Venus didn't feel as if she had her best game going. Later, she would admit she was worried. "I lost a lot of speed on my serve in the middle set," she said. "I definitely didn't feel good at that point. We were both doing a lot of running. I was moving her and she was moving me. I'm sure she was tired. She was breathing hard, struggling to get shots."

But Hingis seemed to get a second wind in the final set. Venus began to run into an old problem — cramps — and Hingis knew it. "It was a tremendous match, especially in the third set," she said. "I tried to keep her running. I knew she was cramping."

Midway through the final set it began to look as if Venus would need a miracle to win. She was still cramping and moving poorly. She still had hope, but Hingis was just making too many good shots. The eighteen-year-old from Switzerland closed it out at 6–3 to end the dream of an all-Williams final. In so doing, she handed Venus the most disappointing defeat of her entire career.

"I've never seen Venus that down," her sister said after the match. "She was so bummed. She felt so bad because her legs had totally given out. She was really down, and that encouraged me to be even tougher out there."

Venus felt she had let everyone down — herself, her sister, her parents, tennis fans, everyone. Yet she tried to put on a brave face and encourage her sister. "Now [Serena's] playing for two people," Venus said. "Hopefully, I gave Martina a good workout today."

So the stage was set for the final, Serena versus Martina Hingis. Experience was definitely on Hingis's side. She had already won five Grand Slam singles titles. But Serena had power and confidence. It was expected to be a great match.

8
A Champion, Then a Crisis

The championship match of the 1999 U.S. Open was played on Sunday, September 12. Both players looked solid right from the first. But as well as Martina Hingis played, Serena seemed to play just that much better. She was stronger, quicker, hit harder, and served rockets. She went after Hingis with an all-court attack that had her opponent reeling. No matter what Hingis tried, Serena had an answer. She won the first set 6–3.

A great champion like Martina Hingis doesn't surrender easily. She continued to play steady tennis, and Serena began making some errors. The second set was a battle. Finally, Serena moved out to a 5–3 advantage. She was one game away from the title, with Hingis serving. Serena took the lead in the game and brought it to match point. Hingis fought it off. Then there was another match point. Again, Hingis won the point — and finally the game. When they battled to 6–6, necessitating a tiebreaker, fans wondered if Serena would be able to close it out.

In the seven-point tiebreaker Serena called on her power once again. Huge serves and powerful ground strokes kept Hingis on the defensive. With the score 6–4 in the tiebreaker, Serena took a deep breath, tossed the ball high over her head, and slammed a hard serve. Hingis took a quick step to her left and stroked a backhand. Serena began to move over for it, then stood and watched it go long. She had won the tiebreaker, 7–4, and the set, 7–6. More important, she had won the match. She was the U.S. Open champion!

Knowing she had won, Serena cried "Oh, my God" as she dropped to her knees and covered her face with her hands. When she was presented with the trophy, she looked at it and said, "That's my name right there, Serena Williams," and she smiled broadly as she carried it around the court.

Venus was watching the whole scene with her parents in the guest box. It hadn't been easy. She was the older sister who had shown the way. Serena had always followed her. Yet Serena had reached the pinnacle first.

It was a historic victory. Serena was the first African-American woman to win the Open since Althea Gibson won her second straight in 1958. Serena said she was happy Gibson had lived long enough to see it happen again. After the match, she received a congratulatory phone call from President Bill Clinton and his daughter, Chelsea. "I'm pretty stoked," she told him.

A day after winning the singles title, Serena teamed with her sister to win the Open doubles crown.

The only thing that tempered the family celebration was the fact that Venus didn't make the finals. After the sisters won the doubles title, those at the press conference said that Venus sat quietly and stared at the floor as twelve of the first fourteen questions related to Serena's singles victory. Finally, a reporter asked Venus whether winning the doubles title took the edge off her singles disappointment. "It doesn't help at all," was her quick answer. "It never helps. I'll never forget it. I'm very bitter."

Anyone who knew the Williams family knew that Venus wasn't having a problem with Serena's success. If she couldn't win, there was no one better than her sister. What was bothering her was the fact that she had reached the final two years earlier and still hadn't been able to take that last big step. As the big sister, she had always led the way. In the natural flow of things, she would have won a Grand Slam singles final first. So the disappointment came from the competitor inside her.

Otherwise, the world seemed to be at the sisters' feet. Venus was now the number-three-ranked player in the world. Serena had moved up to number four. On the court they were playing what was described as an "in-your-face" game punctuated by a combination of athleticism and power that had never before been seen in women's tennis. In addition, both were supremely confident. Serena said, without bragging, "I think everyone I play is intimidated by me." Then, appearing with Jay Leno on *The Tonight Show* shortly after the U.S. Open, she again expressed the confidence she and her sister had. "Other people say they're confident, but they're really not," she told the host. "We say it and we mean it. We know how to get what we want."

There was no question that they had become the most marketable duo in tennis. Not only were they role models for other African-Americans, but as one story said, "Their appeal crosses age, gender, and racial lines." At the 1999 Lipton championships there was a booth set up by tournament organizers so that people could have their hair beaded like Venus and Serena.

In addition, Venus was about to launch a new line of Reebok clothing, starting with a one-shoulder tennis dress she designed herself. She was also featured prominently in a new ad campaign for American Express. It still amazed people how well rounded and self-confident the sisters were. Both could speak several languages, had their high school diplomas, and were planning to take fashion design courses at the Art Institute of Fort Lauderdale, Florida, in the fall.

They had also purchased a ten-acre plot of land about ten miles from their parents' home in Palm Beach Gardens, Florida. They planned to build their own home there. In some ways, things couldn't be better.

Mary Carillo, a former pro and now a TV tennis analyst, was one person who felt they could only get better. "They're both still in diapers in terms of Grand Slam competition," Carillo said. "Watching them grow now reminds me a little bit of coaching adolescent boys. All of a sudden they're growing these new muscles and they want to use them. Venus and Serena have so much power, and sometimes they go to it just because they have it. But I think maybe the casual fan doesn't understand how much court sense they've picked up in the last couple of years; how they've become thinkers on the court."

After the U.S. Open, both sisters flew to Munich, Germany, for the Grand Slam Cup, a big tournament in which the women's singles champion takes home a prize of $800,000. Venus was the defending champion, and all the top players were entered. When the semifinals round rolled around, it was a carbon copy of the U.S. Open. Serena would play Lindsay Davenport, while Venus would face Martina Hingis.

In the first semifinals, Serena showed she was still on a roll. She defeated Davenport easily, 6–3, 6–4, in just seventy-three minutes. Next came Venus and Martina Hingis. They engaged in an epic battle that lasted two hours and thirty-one minutes. Venus won the first set handily, 6–2, her power game seeming to set Hingis back on her heels. When she took a 4–1 lead in the second set it looked like a repeat of her sister's match, a quick straight sets victory.

But a true champion never quits. Hingis suddenly found her game and, as Venus began making unforced errors, won four straight games to take a 5–4 lead in the set. Over one stretch, she won ten of eleven points. Finally, the set went to a tiebreaker. Hingis won it, 8–6, and the set, 7–6. Now the match was even. If Venus wanted to join her sister in the finals, she would have to raise up her game once more.

The third set was almost a reverse of the second. This time Hingis started quickly and raced to a 4–1 lead. It was beginning to look as if the entire pattern of the Open would be repeated. But Venus began fighting like a tiger, hitting with power and chasing down Hingis's attempts to pass her. She evened the set at 4–4, then dropped her serve to trail 5–4. Hingis would be serving for the match.

At one point, Hingis was two points away from winning, but Venus stopped her with a pair of ground stroke winners. Venus eventually won the game, and the two continued to slug it out. This was a tournament in which the final set could not be determined with a tiebreaker. The two had to play until one had a two-game advantage.

The score reached 8–7 in Venus's favor, with Hingis trying to tie it. This time Venus was determined to close it out. She chased down everything her opponent hit at her and raced to a 40–0 lead. She wasted no time, winning it on the very first one. She had done it, 6–2, 6–7, 9–7.

"I was down, I didn't want to lose," Venus said. "I wanted to come out the victor for once."

Someone asked her if this was revenge for Hingis beating her at the Open. "I don't believe in revenge," Venus said, without smiling. "No matter what happened, I still lost at the U.S. Open."

Everyone would be treated to another all-

Williams final. It would be Venus against Serena once again. Serena continued her winning streak and beat her older sister for the first time. The scores were 6–1, 3–6, 6–3. Serena had succeeded her sister as Grand Slam Cup champion, continuing on her great roll that started at the U.S. Open.

"I'd never actually beaten Venus," Serena said. "I didn't know how it feels. It's kind of tough for me to take this win."

It was apparent that neither sister enjoyed beating the other. Venus called it "a win-win situation. One daughter is going to win. What's the difference?"

If there was a strong sense of competition between them, they masked it very well. Neither liked to lose, and whenever one did, she was disappointed. It didn't matter if the opponent was Davenport, Hingis, or Williams. It still hurt. But there obviously wasn't the same sense of satisfaction in beating each other that they felt when they defeated someone else. They were still each other's best friend.

What a year 1999 had been! Venus had won six singles titles, Serena five. They had also added a number of doubles titles, and each had won more than $2 million in prize money. The year, however, did not end on a happy note. In November, Venus acknowledged that her wrists had been bothering her for some time, and the pain had finally gotten so bad she had to see a doctor. He diagnosed her with tendinitis in both wrists. The only way it would go away was with rest.

Suddenly, Venus was off the circuit. As the 2000 season started, she was still on the sidelines. Serena was left to carry on. Then, to the surprise of many, she began losing. For the first time since they had joined the Tour, the Williams sisters were facing a dual crisis: injury and losing.

9
Wimbledon 2000

By the end of March 2000, a question began cropping up throughout the tennis world. What had happened to the supposed domination of the Williams sisters? The way they were both playing at the time of the U.S. Open and Grand Slam Cup had made them appear almost unbeatable. But three months into the year, Venus was still sidelined with tendinitis, having already withdrawn from six tournaments in 2000. Now Serena's game looked as if it was coming apart.

It was a development no one had expected. Serena had injured a knee in February but continued playing. In early March she lost a match in straight sets to Australian Elena Likhoviseva, a player she should have beaten easily. Two weeks later she took a 6–2, 6–1 beating from Mary Pierce at Indian Wells. Then, at the end of the month she made seventy-seven unforced errors in a loss to Jennifer Capriati in the fourth round of the Ericsson Open.

To make matters worse, stories began to circulate that Venus was considering retirement at the age of nineteen. Richard Williams had said a number of times that tennis was the fourth most important thing in his daughters' lives. There was family, then religion (mother and daughters are Jehovah's Witnesses), education, and finally tennis. It wasn't inconceivable that Venus might decide to concentrate on fashion design or some other career.

As usual, Mr. Williams didn't clear anything up with his statements. "She's considering [retirement] very seriously," he told a reporter at Key Biscayne, Florida, at the end of March. "On a scale of ten, I'd say she's a seven or a seven and a half [to retire]. She has been playing a long time now, and she needs time off to rest. She needs to get more education.

"She has enough money now for sure. She has some unbelievable investments paying off very well. She's in a great position right now. If Venus retired from tennis, she'd be making a statement. That's why it's time to walk away. I've seen too many black athletes come out of the ghetto and earn all that money, and four or five years later they're broke and no one cares who they once were."

Then Richard Williams added, "Because of the planning we've done with these two girls, they don't need tennis any longer. When they're thirty years old, they'll have had ten or twelve businesses. The things they'll be doing when they're out of tennis will surpass tennis so much."

There was certainly a great deal of truth in much of what Mr. Williams said. There had been many athletes who reveled in their fame and spent all their money. When it ended, they had nowhere to turn. But Richard and Brandi Williams had certainly prepared their daughters well. There was no doubt of that.

The one thing that Mr. Williams might have overlooked, however, was the competitive fires that burned within Venus and Serena. They were still teens and had not reached their full potential on the court. In addition, Venus had not yet won a Grand Slam title. All top tennis players had that as a goal. It was hard to see Venus retiring yet. Even Serena said she would be surprised if Venus retired. "I expect to see her back and competing soon," she said.

Then, in early April, Serena joined her sister on the injured list. She was playing in the opening round of the Bausch & Lomb Championships at Amelia Island, Florida, against Paola Suarez. Serena wasn't playing well, wasn't moving the way she usually did. She was behind in the match, 3–6, 6–4, 2–5, just one game away from losing. Then, during a changeover, she indicated she couldn't continue.

Doctors diagnosed the problem as patellar tendinitis in the left knee. For Serena, too, the prescription was rest.

Finally, it was time for the French Open. Venus announced she would return to action in a quest for that elusive Grand Slam. With so little match time in the past six months, however, few thought she could win. Then, just seventy-two hours before the start of play, the Williams family had another announcement. Venus was in, but Serena was out. A recurrence of her knee injury forced her to withdraw.

Venus was glad to return. "I knew I would be back eventually," she said. "I had a lot to do and actually ran out of time with everything else that I was doing. But it wasn't very hard. I knew I would be back. It just took longer than I expected."

Asked about the retirement rumors, Venus scoffed. "Lots of reports came out," she said, "but it was just another false alarm."

When Venus took to the court for the French Open, her trademark beaded braids were gone for the first time in her career. "You know, I'm getting older," she said, "and I think it was time for a change. Things happen and here I am."

She also admitted that she was tense on the court because of her lack of playing time over the last six months. "Actually, I think my attitude is too serious right now," she said. "Before, I was very serious but more loose. Here, I feel a lot more pressed for some reason, and I feel more like a perfectionist. I want everything perfect, and when it's not, I feel really awful. I want to get back to the way I was before."

At the beginning, everything appeared to be perfect. In her first several matches, Venus looked sharp. Clay was not her best surface, but she won her first four matches without losing a set. Now she was in the quarterfinals. For a player sidelined for six months, she was looking good enough to possibly win. Her next opponent would be Arantxa Sanchez-Vicario, one of the best clay court players in the world.

That's where Venus's run ended. The Spanish star had too much court savvy and, as usual, returned much of what Venus threw at her, finally winning the match.

Asked if her loss was due to a lack of match practice, she said, "I think so, because each shot I have to think about. Under any normal conditions, I don't have to think about my shots. It's like every shot, especially on the serve. I thought she played very well. What can I say? I think the score tells the story of the whole match."

But what other story did it tell? Had Venus lost the edge? Or was it simply a lack of being match-tough that caused her to lose? Fortunately, her wrists were fine. There was no sign of the tendinitis. All she could do now was regroup and get ready for the next Grand Slam event — Wimbledon.

When Wimbledon began in late June, both Williams sisters were ready to play. Serena had recovered from her knee injury, and Venus had been practicing steadily with no ill effects. Both were fit and ready for runs at the singles and doubles titles. On the fast grass surface, they might be difficult to stop. Venus was seeded fifth, Serena eighth.

Sure enough, both sisters came out with fire in their eyes. They were back to power tennis, combining it with speed, anticipation, great court coverage, and booming serves. They raced through the early rounds, and the anticipation grew. If they both continued to win, they would meet each other in the semifinals.

Serena had an easy road to the semis, rolling over her opponents. She lost just thirteen games in five matches and didn't drop a single set. She seemed primed for a real run at the title. Venus had a tougher road. She had already been taken to three sets once in the early rounds, then had a showdown meeting with Martina Hingis in the quarterfinals. Hingis was the top seed, and Venus knew, from their previous meetings, that it would be a difficult battle. Once again, she was right.

As usual, these rivals engaged in an epic confrontation. Venus finished the match in fine fashion, slamming a blazing ace past the lunging Hingis for the win. Their three sets had taken two hours and thirteen minutes.

The Williams sisters prepared to meet again. Venus knew it would be a hard match. "The most exciting thing is that we're both here, and the biggest challenge is that Serena is extremely powerful and extremely dangerous. And she knows everything I know."

Serena also expected a battle. "I just have to make sure that I play very well because Venus gets a lot of balls back," she said. "She gets everything back, so I have to make sure that I can stick in there."

Both indicated it was going to be a very competitive match, and both wanted to win.

Said Venus, "I just hope that I'll be able to play

better than her. She's really been blazing past her opponents. No mercy. I want to go in with the same attitude."

Serena put it this way. "Venus has to have a lot of confidence now, beating the number-one player in the world. I'm just going to have to see her as another opponent, and I'm sure she will, too. But most of all, I think we're going to go out there and actually enjoy ourselves and have a really good time."

Venus added the final touch. "Everyone wants to win Wimbledon," she said. "It doesn't matter if I'm playing Serena or I'm playing Pete Sampras. I'm going to want to win Wimbledon."

Both sisters played their usual brand of power tennis, but neither had that fine edge that would make her play brilliant. It was more a matter of who would make the fewest errors. As one report put it, "[It was a match] dominated by errors rather than spectacular winners."

In the first set, Venus was steadier. Serena was hitting the ball hard, but many of her forehand blasts were sailing long. Venus won the set easily, 6–2. In the second, Serena dug in and fought harder. Neither could take charge, and at 6–6, they had to play a crucial tiebreaker. Serena took a 3–1 lead, and for a moment, it looked as if the match would go to a third set. But then Serena began making forehand errors again. Venus won the last six points, and the match ended on a double fault by Serena. Big sister had won, 6–2, 7–6. She was in the Wimbledon final.

As soon as the final point was decided, Venus walked slowly to the net. She didn't jump for joy, didn't smile. In fact, her expression was downright disappointed. She shook hands with her sister, then put her arm around her shoulder as they walked off. Despite the cheers, Venus managed just a halfhearted wave to the crowd. The two sisters didn't even give the traditional curtsy to the royal box. There was simply no joy in this victory.

"It's not really so much fun," Venus said. "If it was a final it would have been different, but it was a semifinal and I hate to see Serena go. Hopefully, it'll be like the U.S. Open and I'll follow through and rebound for Williams."

Serena was in tears as she shook the chair umpire's hand. She was still wiping away tears a half hour after the match.

"I just didn't play well today, it just didn't go right for me," she said. "Venus played pretty well today and she brought out her best game against me and I guess I wasn't all that ready. I expected to play a lot better than I did today. It was my goal to do better. I'm only eighteen, Venus is twenty. I've got a lot of years ahead of me."

It hadn't been easy for Richard Williams, either. He couldn't even watch. During the match he walked the streets near the stadium. "I was crying when I heard Serena lost," he said. "This was too emotional for me. I didn't sleep last night. I kept trying to go to sleep so finally I had to stay up and read. [Serena's] my baby, that's the last child that was born to me. I felt sympathy for Serena, very much so, very much so. Serena was very sad and disappointed because she felt she should have won. Serena hates losing. Nothing bothers Serena more than to lose."

Venus was so upset that it almost seemed it would be difficult for her to get up for the final. She couldn't stop talking about her sister. "I'm always the big sister," she said. "I always take care of Serena no matter what. . . . I'm always worried about her. [But] she's a competitor, probably more than I am, and she hates to lose. We just have to go for it in doubles."

Despite the emotion of beating her sister, Venus still had one more match to play. Her opponent was a familiar one, Lindsay Davenport. Davenport had also had injury problems early in the year, and once the match started, it quickly became apparent that Venus's combination of speed and power was too much for her. Serving beautifully and banging winners from both sides, Venus took the first set in just thirty-two minutes, winning it, 6–3. But the second set was a different story.

Both players were obviously getting tired, and the errors began. It was as if both were trying too hard. Venus's extra speed and her strategy of moving Davenport around kept her in the set. Finally, as in the match with Serena, the score was tied at 6–6, and it went to a tiebreaker.

That's when Davenport seemed to lose it. She made four unforced errors and found herself down 5–1. Venus was two points from realizing her dream. Davenport won the next point, but then Venus ran it to 6–2 with another winner. Match point. Davenport saved one with a service winner, but on the next point, she hit a backhand into the net. It was over. Venus had won the tiebreaker, 7–3, and had taken the match, 6–3, 7–6. She had done it. She had won her first Grand Slam. She was the Wimbledon champion!

10
Athletes for Our Time

Venus's reaction to her Wimbledon win was completely opposite that of her semifinals win over Serena. As soon as Davenport netted the final point, Venus leaped and twirled in the air as she made her way to the net. After shaking hands with her opponent, she bounded up the stairs that led to the friends' box and embraced her sister, as if she had won for both of them. Then she slapped hands with her father before returning to the court.

"This was meant to be," Venus said. "I worked real hard all my life. I had a lot of sacrifices."

Just as her sister was the first African-American woman to win the U.S. Open since Althea Gibson in 1958, Venus was the first African-American woman to win Wimbledon since Althea Gibson in that same year, 1958. Venus showed that she was well aware of the historical significance of her win.

Speaking of Gibson as well as of 1990 finalist Zina Garrison, Venus said, "It had to be hard because people were unable to see past color. Still, these days, it's hardly any different because you realize it's been only forty years. How can you change centuries of being biased in forty years? There have been so few black people to win Wimbledon or even just to play outstanding tennis. So hopefully there will be more. Naturally, we're going to do our best to change that. We already have."

When people said the Williams sisters transcended tennis, they were right. Most twenty-year-olds would not be thinking that way after winning one of the most prestigious tennis tournaments in the world. Venus, however, knew it was more than serves, backhands, and passing shots. She was well aware of the ways of the world, as well as the Williams sisters' roles in helping to change things.

Former champion Billie Jean King pointed out the importance of the Williams sisters' success and the way they had handled it. "Venus and Serena certainly have grabbed the imagination and hearts of people in a way that crosses all color barriers," King said. "Hopefully, for children of color in particular, [the Williamses' success] would interest them and light a fire in their belly. Althea Gibson couldn't even play in a sanctioned tournament until 1950. The first thing I thought when Venus won was, 'Althea would have loved to be here today.' It would have been great."

Despite the celebration that followed Venus's win, the girls weren't finished yet. They joined forces to win the doubles crown as well. In the final, they defeated Ai Sugiyama and Julie Halard-Decugis, 6–3, 6–2. It was their third Grand Slam doubles title. After this one, they acted more like excited young girls who loved tennis.

"We're both going to try to get as much as we can," Venus said.

Added Serena, "We're both really greedy."

When someone reminded them that Venus had missed six months to injury and Serena two, the younger sister nodded. "It's really amazing for us to come back like this," Serena said. "People are going to practice harder to beat us. But you know what? We are, too. We mean business. We can do a lot better. We're not playing our best tennis right now. There's a lot of room for improvement."

Both attended the champions' dinner and ball, wearing specially designed sleeveless gowns and looking like beautiful young women who were also determined athletes. Wimbledon had been a rousing success, especially after the injury problems earlier in the year. Now it was time to look to the future.

Most people now thought that the sisters were ready to do what their father had predicted all along — become the two top-ranked players in the world. Both admitted it was their goal.

"Definitely, it's a personal goal," Venus said. "We both really want to be number one. We've had a few hurdles to jump, we're on our way, we believe in ourselves. Next year we start with the Australian Open and the French."

Serena added, "We can basically beat all the players out there, and we are now playing a little bit more consistently."

The thought of the sisters getting much better has to be frightening for the rest of the players on the Tour. Following a short break after Wimbledon, the sisters were back in action, prepping for the U.S. Open in September. Venus got back in action at the Bank of the West Classic in California and promptly beat Davenport again in the finals. From there she went to the Acura Classic, also in California, and topped Monica Seles in the final.

Serena returned to tournament play at the ESTYLE.COM Classic in Los Angeles and wound up beating Davenport in the final. Venus and Serena had now won four straight tournaments and hadn't lost to anyone except each other in twenty-nine straight matches.

"We're just trying to go one match at a time, one tournament at a time, until we can get the top spots," Serena said. "We're going for it."

The only thing keeping the sisters from being numbers one and two were their early season injuries. By missing so many sanctioned Tour events, they didn't have enough computer points to earn the top spots. But in the minds of nearly everyone, including the players, they had become the best. Lindsay Davenport, who had recently lost to both sisters, compared their games. "They hit the ball hard and serve very well," Davenport said. "They're tough. They have a lot of similarities to their game. Right now, Venus is more consistent. Serena was more consistent last summer. They both have such dangerous games."

Martina Hingis added her sentiments. "Venus moves better than Serena," she said. "Serena serves better. Both are fun to play. Venus plays more of a mental game, lulls you into a rally and then puts it away. Serena just goes for every shot."

The third week in August, Serena was at the Du Maurier Open at Montreal and fought her way into the finals against Martina Hingis. In the second set, Serena began to limp, favoring her left foot.

Moving into the third set, Serena was obviously in pain. She limped through the first three games, which Hingis won, then had to retire. The medical report said she had sesamoiditis — an inflammation of a small bone on the base of her left foot. Because her foot was bothering her, Serena had been trying to hit winners on every shot. She led Hingis in aces, 10–0, in winners, 32–3, and in unforced errors, 33–9. "That's the way I think I should play from now on," she said, "as if I've been injured, so I can keep playing like that."

Fortunately, by the time the U.S. Open rolled around, Serena was once again fit to play. She would be defending the title she had won the year before. In the eyes of most experts, her biggest competition would come from her sister. Venus went into the Open with a 19-match winning streak.

Most of the talk around Arthur Ashe Stadium was of a Williams–Williams final. No one, experts said, could handle the power, speed, and athleticism of Venus and Serena. They seemed destined to be one and two in the world. The only question that remained was, which sister would be number one?

Because of Serena's position in the draw, she

had to meet defending champion Lindsay Davenport in the quarterfinals. Davenport had the power to match strokes with Serena, but didn't have her speed. Early in the match, however, it was apparent that Davenport was really on her game . . . and Serena wasn't. Lindsay was hitting deep, moving the ball around, catching the lines on her passing shots. Serena was just missing, making too many unforced errors and not winning the key points.

The first set was on serve at 4–4 when Davenport finally broke Serena. With a 5–4 lead, she served out the first set, winning 6–4. The huge crowd expected Serena to rally and turn it around in the second set. It didn't happen. Davenport continued to play great tennis and closed out the second set and the match, 6–2. Suddenly, Serena was eliminated. There was no hope for an all-Williams final.

After the match, Serena made no excuses. She lost. Yet when asked if there would be a Williams–Williams final in a Grand Slam someday, she didn't waver.

"I'm sure a lot of people never want to see an all-Williams final," she said. "It's going to happen in the future inevitably. Nobody's going to be able to stop it. Unfortunately, I didn't pull my end up this year. I'm going to do my utmost to make sure it happens . . . because that's just what I would like."

Venus moved through her quarterfinal match and had to play Martina Hingis in the semis. Before the match, a story broke that Hingis and Davenport had talked about doing whatever they could to prevent the Williams sisters from both reaching the final.

"I think everyone was expecting an all-Williams final," said Davenport. "Martina and I had a little talk — we didn't want it to happen."

When Venus squared off with Hingis in the semifinal, she fought her way through three tough sets before winning the match. She was in the final.

After the match, Venus was asked what kept her going, especially when she was behind in the deciding set.

"I just kept slugging, fighting away," she said. "I've got a big heart these days. I really didn't want to lose. I felt this was my opportunity. I deserve to be in the finals and I just needed to get it done."

In the final, Venus would face the woman who had beat her sister. Lindsay Davenport had won her semifinal against Russian Elena Dementieva, and now had the opportunity to beat both Williams sisters in a Grand Slam event. It was also the first U.S. Open final in twenty-one years between two American-born women.

The match was described as the hardest-hitting women's final in U.S. Open history. Both players were blasting shots from both sides. Early on, it was all Davenport. Lindsay raced to a 4–1 lead in the opening set before Venus began putting her game back together. She began finding the corners with passing shots and blasting her own service winners. Venus reeled off five straight games to take the first set, 6–4.

The second set was also tough. Venus had to

stave off a number of break points, and continued to handle Davenport's serves well. She won the set and the match, 7–5, to succeed Serena as U.S. Open champion. It was another happy celebration for the Williams clan as father Richard came down on the court and did a little victory dance. Serena, looking a bit wistful, yelled out, "Great job, Venus."

Venus was the star of the show. Her serves, her stamina, even her outfit — an orange sherbet halter dress, sparkling choker, and shimmering earrings — set her apart. Afterward, she spoke about how far her game had come since her first finals appearance in 1997.

"I have no regrets [about] 1997 because I just — I didn't know what I was doing, basically. I was just a yearling. I think I'm a different competitor [now] than what I was in the past. For me, it didn't matter that I was down 4–1. I was just competing. I've always felt like the best player. I think it's all an attitude, kind of the attitude you take out there toward your game."

Venus had won Wimbledon and the U.S. Open in the same year, which was not an easy feat. Even though the computer rankings still showed Hingis at number one, everyone, even Lindsay Davenport, conceded that Venus was the best.

It was no surprise, then, when Venus was selected as one of the athletes who would represent the United States at the 2000 Olympic Games, held in Sydney, Australia. Serena was picked to play on the U.S. women's doubles team with her sister. Not surprisingly, the Williamses were favorites to win gold medals in both events. And they didn't disappoint.

In singles, Venus continued on the roll that had brought her the Wimbledon and U.S. Open championships. She moved easily through the early rounds, and defeated Monica Seles in the semifinals, then won the gold medal by beating Russia's Elena Dementieva, 6–2, 6–4. The victory brought her winning streak up to thirty-two straight matches. In doubles, the sisters mowed down the rest of the field. In the gold medal match they easily defeated Miriam Oremans and Kristie Boogert, 6–1, 6–1. As doubles partners, the Williams sisters are beginning to look unbeatable.

Both Venus and Serena thoroughly enjoyed their Olympic experience and were gracious in victory. "This is much more meaningful than I thought," Venus said, after her singles triumph. "I felt really emotional. I felt really excited. It was just really one moment in time, because you see it on TV, how the competitor bows their head, and they put the medal on. It was really great. It was me."

"It has been fantastic here," Serena added. "Just to win the gold medal, it has been a great thing for me and my family. We've worked so hard. It's great for everyone, for the whole U.S. team."

It stands to reason that injuries are now the only thing that can slow the Williams sisters. Their talent level is rising above that of everyone else. At the same time, the way they play, the power they generate, and the speed they have open them up for injury, especially when the pounding is on hard courts. If they stay healthy, they may become the best of all time.

Venus and Serena Williams have certainly shown they are great tennis players, but they are also well-rounded, confident individuals. They have continued to educate themselves and are totally aware of their heritage and the history surrounding it.

Most important, they are happy. In many ways, they have been typical teens as they made their way up the tennis rankings. Their parents raised them the right way, helping the girls become interesting individuals.

Venus enjoys many different activities off the court. Among her favorite movies are *The Shawshank Redemption, Tommy Boy, Coneheads, Mildred Pierce, Alice Doesn't Live Here Anymore,* and *Mahogany.* Her favorite musical groups are Green Day, Toadies, Our Lady Peace, and Rancid. She also loves to listen to the Jackson Five.

Some of her other interests are studying Russian history and Chinese culture, reading almost anything, and working toward an associate's degree in fashion design. She loves Swedish, English, and French antique furniture and wants to speak five languages — English, French, Italian, German, and Russian.

Venus also enjoys surfing and has two dogs, Starr and Pete. Pete is a Yorkshire terrier who travels with her to all corners of the world.

Serena, on the other hand, is more carefree. She enjoys surfing and skateboarding in her spare time. Also a reader, her favorite author is poet and novelist Maya Angelou. She has talked about becoming an actress someday and loves to play the guitar. She also enjoys speaking to students and conducting tennis clinics for minorities.

Sometimes it's hard to believe that so much has happened to the Williams sisters in such a short time. They have become two of the most popular and recognizable athletes in the world. Their potential as tennis players is unlimited. Perhaps the most difficult thing they will face in upcoming years is having to play each other in Grand Slam events. They are two sisters who hate to lose, but they also hate to play and beat each other.

They have already left a huge mark on their sport, as African-Americans, as sisters, and as young women from an uncommon tennis background. They have changed tennis with their style, their talent, and their attitude. Their greatest impact was best described by former tennis champion Chris Evert when she said, "Tennis has always been a rich man or woman's sport, but now Venus and Serena can change tennis, just like Tiger Woods has done in golf. They've shown that no matter what the color of your skin or how rich you are, you can become a success."